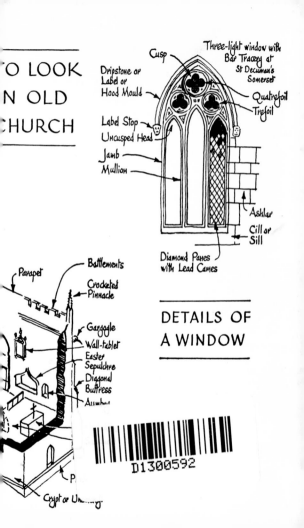

O LOOK
N OLD
CHURCH

Three-light window with Bar Tracery at St Decuman's Somerset

Cusp

Dripstone or Label or Hood Mould

Quatrefoil

Trefoil

Label Stop

Uncusped Head

Jamb

Mullion

Ashlar

Cill or Sill

Diamond Panes with Lead Cames

DETAILS OF A WINDOW

Parapet

Battlements

Crocketed Pinnacle

Gargoyle

Wall-tablet

Easter Sepulchre

Diagonal Buttress

Aumbry

P

Crypt or Undercroft

D1300592

THE OBSERVER'S
POCKET SERIES

. . .

THE OBSERVER'S BOOK OF
OLD ENGLISH CHURCHES

The Observer Books

The Observer's Book of

OLD ENGLISH
CHURCHES

LAWRENCE E. JONES, F.S.A.

Describing the principal
EXTERIOR & INTERIOR FEATURES
with 44 plates from photographs
and text drawings by A. S. B. NEW

FREDERICK WARNE & CO LTD
FREDERICK WARNE & CO INC
LONDON · NEW YORK

LIBRARY OF CONGRESS CATALOG
CARD NO. 65-15723

ISBN 0 7232 0078 5
Printed in Great Britain by
Cox & Wyman Ltd, London, Fakenham and Reading
743. 676

ALPHABETICAL LIST OF CONTENTS

v

vi

ARCHITECTURAL PERIODS

Saxon	7th century to 1066			
Norman	1066	to	1189	Romanesque
Transitional Norman	1145	to	1189	
Early English	1189	to	1280	
Decorated	1280	to	1377	Gothic
Perpendicular	1377	to	1547	
Early Tudor	1500	to	1547	
Late Tudor	1547	to	1603	
Stuart (Jacobean 1603 to 1625, Carolean 1625 to 1649)	1603	to	1689	Renaissance
Hanoverian (William and Mary, Anne and Georgian)	1689	to	1837	Classical

ACKNOWLEDGMENTS

(*Please note where Plate references are given a = 1, b = 2, c = 3 and d = 4*)

The author wishes to thank all those who have kindly given consent to reproduce their photographs.

A special debt of gratitude is due to the photographers responsible for the colour plates, namely Dr T. E. Allibone, C.B.E., F.R.S., for Pl. 4a, the late Rev. Canon T. P. Backhouse for Pls. 1b, 2b and 3a, Mr Alfred Proctor for Pls. 1a, 2a and 3b, Mr Edward B. Talbot for Pl. 4b and Mr Christopher G. Bubb for the jacket illustration.

Of the monochrome illustrations, Canon Backhouse is also responsible for Pls. 7b and c, 8b and d, 17d, 21c, 24b, 27c, 28d, 34c, 36d and 42b and d, Mr Proctor for Pls. 9c and d, 19d, 27d and 29d, and Mr Talbot for Pls. 8a, 9a, 11b, 12b, 13c, 14b and d, 29c and 34d.

Pls. 25a and 28b are the Royal Commission on Historical Monuments photographs and are reproduced by permission of the Controller of H.M. Stationery Office.

Mr A. F. Kersting has provided forty illustrations, namely nos. 5b and d, 6a, 7a, 9b, 10a and b, 11c and d, 13d, 14a, 15c, 16d, 17a, 19a, 20b, 21b, 24a, 25c, 26b and d, 27b, 29b, 30b, 31c, 32a, 33a, b and c, 35a, 36b and c, 37b, 38b and d, 39a, b and d, 40b and 42c.

Mr Reece Winstone is the photographer in respect of Pls. 6c, 12c, 18d, 22a, b and c, 37c, 38c, 40a, 41d and 44b and c, and Mr Walter Mathers of Pl. 24d.

Messrs B. T. Batsford Ltd have kindly allowed the reproduction of Pls. 17b, 23c, 25d, 28a, 30a, 34a and 35d from the collection of the late Mr B. C. Clayton.

Pls. 10d, 20c, 23b, 32d, 34b, 36a and 41c are from the collection of the late Mr F. H. Crossley and are reproduced by kind permission of Mrs Crossley.

The author is also indebted to the late Dr Frank Butler for Pl. 15a, Mr Robert Sherlock for Pl. 43a, and Mr P. S. Spokes, F.S.A., for Pl. 37a.

Pls. 12d and 13b are from photographs by Mr Niall

Maddock, and Pls. 5a, 10c, 12a and 16a are from photographs by the author.

Pl. 16c is from the photograph by Mr Anthony S. B. New, F.R.I.B.A., A.M.I.STRUCT.E., of the firm of Messrs Seely and Paget, and the writer is deeply grateful to him for all the text drawings which he has drawn specially for this book, and which are invaluable in making the subject clear to the reader. His front endpaper makes a most fitting beginning.

The back endpaper of Somerset towers and the Perpendicular window tracery on page 65 are from Penguin Books' admirable *Buildings of England* Series by Dr Nikolaus Pevsner. The kindness of these publishers in permitting reproduction here is much appreciated.

The illustrations of brasses have been obtained from prints by the Victoria and Albert Museum or from photographs of rubbings in their possession; Pl. 43c is also due to the Museum.

The remaining fifty-three photographs have been obtained from the splendid library of the National Monuments Record at 23 Savile Row, W. 1, where photographs of every church can be studied. The writer gladly records not only their generosity but also the courteous help always given by their staff.

The Rev. M. Moreton, Rector of Exeter St Mary Steps, has been good enough to furnish the particulars about the clock on his church tower.

The illustrations have to be rather small, but if a magnifying glass or epidiascope is used, the result will be most effective.

NEW COUNTY BOUNDARIES

County boundaries were fixed hundreds of years ago mainly by geological strata and by rivers. One could often tell the county by looking at the church, buildings and scenery. The new boundaries ignore such characteristics and are based on population.

250 alterations would be necessary in this book and even then this would not be accurate. Here are two

examples. The finest church towers are in the former county of Somerset. The county of Avon has been formed partly out of Somerset and partly out of Gloucestershire. The reference to the finest towers therefore only applies to a small portion of the new county that was formerly in Somerset. Again Yorkshire is mainly divided into North, South and West. If there was a county of East Yorkshire following the former East Riding all would be well, but it is now included in the new county of Humberside which extends across the river to include North Lincolnshire, where the churches are quite different to the grand ones of the former East Riding. Rutland was a most attractive small county with its very distinctive churches. It is now swallowed up by Leicestershire. The same applies to Huntingdonshire which has been swallowed up by Cambridgeshire. Worcestershire and Herefordshire (again quite different architecturally) are combined in name so that each can still be referred to individually. The same applies to Cumberland and Westmorland but the new county is called Cumbria. Parts of Lancashire have been transferred to the latter county which is indeed appropriate with regard to scenery. The most difficult new boundary is the straight line putting the whole of North Berkshire into Oxfordshire. The other way round would almost have been an improvement geologically as South Oxfordshire is typically Berkshire. Christchurch Priory is now in Dorset and the church is more fitting in that county than in Hampshire.

Many people still refer to the old counties and have little knowledge about the alterations. For the time being, therefore, no alterations have been made in this book, but the above facts should be borne in mind, particularly by young people born in the county of Cleveland who might otherwise think that the book is out-of-date.

INTRODUCTION

Visiting an old church can be enthralling if you know what to observe in it. An Observer book on the subject should therefore bring all points of observation before the tourist so that the meaning of this great heritage of art will no longer be lost to him. Not every church, of course, will have all the features mentioned, but it is hoped that the visitor will learn what to look for and where to find it, and will then know whether it is original or modern. Each church, after all, is built of some material, follows a plan, and at least has a font, benches, pulpit and altar.

Not only are all the different parts of a church and its contents explained, but variations according to date and locality are duly noted. We have tried to keep to the order in which the various details would be seen first on a walk round the outside of the building and then on walking up the church inside to the High Altar at its east end.

Not many people realize the great number of medieval churches still remaining. Nearly every village has its church dating from Norman or even Saxon times. There are indeed no less than ten thousand of medieval foundation in this country.

Wherever one is, there will be something to see. For an amazing day's drive one could not do better than visit the churches around the route from Spalding, Lincs, to King's Lynn, Norfolk. Another such route is between Clare and Hadleigh, Suffolk.

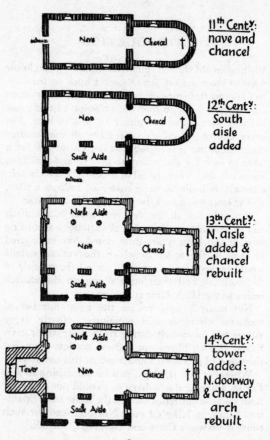

11th Cent?:
nave and
chancel

entrance · Nave · Chancel ✝

12th Cent?:
South
aisle
added

Nave · Chancel ✝
South Aisle
entrance

13th Cent?:
N. aisle
added &
chancel
rebuilt

North Aisle
Nave · Chancel ✝
South Aisle

14th Cent?:
tower
added:
N. doorway
& chancel
arch
rebuilt

North Aisle
Tower · Nave · Chancel ✝
South Aisle

2

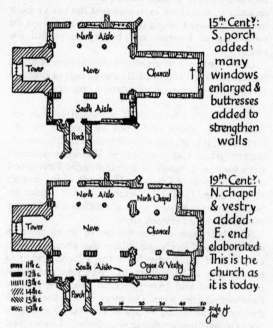

15th Cent?: S. porch added: many windows enlarged & buttresses added to strengthen walls

19th Cent?: N. chapel & vestry added: E. end elaborated: This is the church as it is today.

11th c.
12th c.
13th c.
14th c.
15th c.
19th c.

scale of feet

These plans show the development of a typical church and are based upon Walkern church, Herts; the hatching which indicates the various periods is more or less standard in such key plans

3

Do not, however, visit only the specially notable churches. Every village should be visited that has an ancient church or even one that has been rebuilt but is of ancient foundation; there will always be something of interest and beauty to reward the visitor.

Local features add greatly to the enjoyment of the subject; so often you can tell in what part of England you are by noting certain details, particularly the tower.

Few churches were built immediately after the Reformation (about 1536), but we continue our observations, though more briefly, until the nineteenth century when vast numbers of Victorian churches were built as a result of the Industrial Revolution and the growth of London. The body of the church of Wickham, Berks, is Victorian, but it retains its Saxon tower and there is thus a difference of over a thousand years between them.

The best part of any village or small town is usually around its church. Many churches, however, are situated some way from the village, and it is certain that a "church-crawl" will take one down narrow lanes and byways which one would never have visited otherwise. The more remote the church the more interesting it nearly always is; examples are Orchardleigh, Somerset, Stow, Lincs, and Tixover, Rutland. The small church of Widford, Oxon, surrounded by fields, is an epitome of the history of the English countryside, for it is built on the site of a Roman villa, and a part of the Roman pavement can still actually be seen.

With a car the most remote parish is now accessible, but motorists, even in their holiday area, usually keep to the main road and therefore see little. A turn down any side road, however, will bring you to a village where the real beauty of England will be revealed.

The village church is a summary of village life for hundreds of years: in its Godward aspect one can feel the atmosphere of devotion and worship by the faithful through the centuries; on the human side there are the memorials to those who have lived there since Saxon times and the craftsmanship in wood and stone wrought lovingly by unknown villagers to beautify the House of God.

Inside there will certainly be peace and tranquillity—the best tonic for the rush and noise of today.

Most Englishmen have a sense of history and like to visit old buildings. It is a hobby, moreover, that can be enjoyed all the year round: in fine weather one is able to visit the churches and in bad weather to study illustrations in books on the subject.

Some churches have an admirable guide or notes; others have nothing. The subject is not really a difficult one, and the aim of this book is to be a general guide to any church, so that the observer will be able to appreciate and enjoy all that he observes.

SITUATION

Frequently one's first joy is finding the church at all! Quite often it is some way from the village (Horsmonden, Kent). The Lord of the Manor was usually responsible originally for building the parish church, and he frequently did so on his own land near his house. In East Anglia he often resided in the middle of a large park and the church therefore follows suit. In Northamptonshire and surrounding districts, however, he was more sociable, and his house may actually be in the village street, however large a park there may be at the back; and the church is near by in the street as well. Undoubtedly the site of a church was also sometimes fixed by a prehistoric straight track.

The situation of an old church is frequently delightful. Visitors to Minehead, Somerset, know the church high up on North Hill, with the old thatched cottages climbing up to it. Visitors to the beautiful National Trust gardens of Stourhead, Wilts, will know the glorious situation of Stourton church. Portchester, Hants, is romantically situated in a corner of the old Roman fort.

For examples of church and manor house close together in charming surroundings we can mention Brympton D'Evercy, Somerset, Great Chalfield, Wilts, Wickhamford, Worcs, and Boconnoc, Cornwall. The church and manor house of North Cadbury, Somerset, make a fine picture. At Nevill Holt, Leics, and Wyke Champflower, Somerset, the church is actually built on to the manor house.

Warwickshire can provide some delightful settings as at Merevale, Rowington and Wormleighton.

The North has much grand and beautiful scenery. There are therefore many charming situations for churches, as at Ulpha, Isel and Waberthwaite, Cumberland, Brougham, and Ormside, West-

Plate 1 *above* Lanteglos-by-Fowey, Cornwall, the glory of the West Country with the church tower dominating the landscape.

below Framsden, Suffolk, the charm of the country church. This one is typical of East Anglia.

Plate 2

left Dittisham, Devon, on the River Dart. The lovely medieval stone pulpit.

right Southwold, on the Suffolk coast. Two panels of the beautiful 15th-century screen: St. Andrew and St. Peter.

morland, and Bolam and Brinkburn, Northumberland. In Yorkshire, East Riding, is North Newbald, and in the North Riding are West Tanfield, Grinton and Husthwaite. At Romaldkirk, in the latter county, the village green and handsome church make a beautiful picture. Mungrisdale, Cumberland (Pl. 5), shows well a delightful setting in the North.

The English scene is often "made" by a tall church tower dominating the landscape. The illustration of Lanteglos-by-Fowey, Cornwall (Pl. 1), tries to capture such a typical view.

The most lovely situations are attained in the West Country when the church is near the sea or on a river estuary. We can mention Wembury and St Petrock's, Dartmouth, in Devon, and St Anthony-in-Meneage, Gunwalloe, St Just-in-Roseland, St Winnow and Mylor in Cornwall.

Countisbury, Devon, is very isolated 900 feet up on its Foreland, but there are magnificent views over Lynmouth and this grand coast. At Buckland Brewer, Devon, the church stands high and can be seen for miles around. In the adjoining parish of Littleham, however, the church is tucked away on its own and is barely visible until it is reached.

CHURCHYARD

A churchyard must be centred upon the church, which alone gives meaning to Christian burial; and it must be planned as a whole. It is to be hoped that the grass is kept as a lawn should be and that the headstones are of stone blending with the character of the place.

Entry is usually through a lych-gate, which shelters the coffin and the bearers awaiting the priest who meets them on consecrated ground, and then—representing the Church, which commends the departed to God—leads the procession. Some medieval lych-gates remain; a notable one is at Boughton Monchelsea, Kent, and there is another at Anstey, Herts. Occasionally a picturesque entry is beneath old houses, as at Penshurst, Kent, and in Devon sometimes the ancient Church House adjoins the churchyard, as at Walkhampton, South Tawton and Braunton.

Many headstones of eighteenth-century date have bold lettering and pleasing designs. Good gravestones can be seen at Lyddington, Rutland, where the churchyard adjoins the ancient Bede House.

Epitaphs are often of interest and unintentional humour can occur. When the two usual sentiments "At rest" and "Until we meet again" are expressed together by a nagging widow, their meaning might be misunderstood. It is recorded that a heavy drinker had "This one's on me", and that on another occasion "At last" was carved instead of "At rest."

The churchyard cross dominated every churchyard before the Reformation. It was probably the only memorial to all the dead in the days before gravestones, and a much better idea too, for belief in eternal life with God is rather more important than the desire to be remembered in the sight of men. (Methwold, Norfolk, is an example today.)

In districts where good stone is abundant, medieval remains of such crosses are very common. Occasionally the cross is complete, as at Ampney Crucis, Glos, and Somersby, Lincs. The head contains a rood (a crucifix) on one side and figures of Our Lady and Child on the other side, and this was no doubt the usual arrangement. In the North

Saxon cross.   Churchyard cross.
Eyam, Derbyshire.   Ampney Crucis, Glos.

and in Cornwall, Saxon crosses may be found, well-known examples being at Eyam and Bakewell, Derbyshire, and Bewcastle and Gosforth, Cumberland. The tallest monolith in England is at Rudston, East Riding.

The beauty and antiquity of trees in an English country churchyard are proverbial. The yew is the pre-eminent tree, and although it may have provided bows for archers, its main use was to supply the evergreen which was the special emblem of immortality. It would also undoubtedly have afforded some protection to the fabric from our climate. Many old yew trees, often of immense size and well over 1,000 years old, remain, particularly in the south of England. Magnificent examples are at Darley Dale and Doveridge, Derbyshire, Crowhurst (Surrey and Sussex), Ulcombe, Kent, Tandridge, Surrey, Brockenhurst, Corhampton, South Hayling and Selborne, Hants, and Woolland, Dorset.

If one is at Painswick in Gloucestershire, one cannot resist counting the trimmed yew trees; there are ninety-nine. A fig tree grows out of the church wall at Manaccan, Cornwall.

If a churchyard is circular, it generally indicates a very ancient site; possibly even of a heathen temple. It is most probable that the Christian Church often took over the same site, but placed it "under new management". The Church was always wise enough not to make unnecessary changes, and to this day it allows you to call the days of the week after heathen gods. There are circular churchyards at Lavendon, Bucks, Aldworth, East Hendred and Letcombe Regis, Berks, Wixoe, Suffolk, Steeple Bumpstead, Essex, Stagsden, Beds, and Rudston, East Riding.

The view from the churchyard will often be admired, particularly if the church is on high ground above the village. Examples are numerous, but we must mention Selworthy, Somerset, Kersey, Suffolk, Rockingham, Northants, Goudhurst, Kent, Seend, Wilts, Bow Brickhill and Edlesborough, Bucks,

Shillington, Beds, Horsley, Derbyshire, and Kirkby Lonsdale, Westmorland.

Likewise churches on hills are often landmarks and can be seen for miles around. The tower of Dundry, Somerset, was built as a landmark for shipping in the Bristol Channel. Other churches similarly situated can be found at Rock, Worcs, Holme-on-Spalding-Moor, East Riding, and of course Lincoln and Durham Cathedrals.

MATERIALS

(See map, back endpaper)

Old churches are usually built of local material, which is why they harmonize with the landscape.

The best building stone is oolite stone, a great band of which stretches across the country from Somerset and Dorset to east Yorkshire, giving us the charming grey stone villages of the Cotswolds, the glorious church towers of Somerset, the superb stone spires of Northamptonshire and neighbouring counties, and the grand churches of the East Riding of Yorkshire. Similarly the Fens of west Norfolk abound in magnificent churches as the stone was easily transported from the stone belt by water (Terrington St Clement, Walpole St Peter, Pl. 42, and West Walton, Pl. 11).

In Norfolk and Suffolk (and in chalk country generally) flint is almost the only material used. The stone necessary for doorways, windows and buttresses was carried at great cost and therefore used with strict economy. Combination of the two materials produces the very beautiful ornamentation known as flush-work, which may be on towers (Southwold, Pl. 7, and Eye, Suffolk), porches (Kersey and Framsden, Pl. 1, Suffolk), or cleres-tories (Cavendish and Coddenham, Suffolk). A well-known example is at St Michael Coslany, Norwich. Inscriptions and religious emblems, such as the crowned M for St Mary, often occur in this black-and-white fashion. To produce the

Flush-work. Hawstead, Suffolk.

black colour the flints are knapped or split in half. Often a whole wall or tower may be built of knapped flints, occasionally laboriously cut into squares.

The surface and cores of flints may be black or grey, and these are therefore the predominant colours in East Anglia. Flush-work in that area is usually in thin vertical strips or squares, whereas in Dorset large horizontal strips are common.

In the chalk and clay country of south-east England, absence of good building stone accounts for the many humble village churches. Flints are also used in this area together with chalk. Timber was, however, plentiful for belfries and spires, especially in Sussex and Surrey.

Essex also has many notable examples of timber towers and belfries (see p. 35), and Greensted (Pl. 13) is known far and wide as having the oldest wooden walls in England—Saxon split oak tree trunks. The same county makes full use of delightfully coloured red brickwork, particularly in the Tudor period. Layer Marney church and Hall are certainly a joy to behold, and there are many splendid towers of this material, (see p. 24), as well as porches (Sandon and Feering) and clerestories (Great Baddow) (Pl. 14). A complete church of early sixteenth-century brick (even including the font) is at Chignal Smealy, Essex. Long narrow red bricks are different. They are Roman tiles and were reused by medieval builders.

Running parallel to the North and South Downs is a sandstone ridge, so that churches in those areas are of light yellow sandstone. North of the Chilterns is a belt of reddish brown sandstone. Sandstone is the usual building material in the north-west Midlands, but it weathers badly. The colour may be pink or dull yellow. Around Cheshire there is a local type of half-timber and plaster, black-and-white ("magpie") (Lower Peover and Marton, Pl. 7, and also Melverley, Salop). Around the Pennines a limestone predominates.

In the extreme north-west of England, the building stones are usually of inferior quality and of slaty texture, and the churches are accordingly coarse, but nevertheless they still harmonize with the landscape. (Grasmere, Westmorland, Pl. 9, and Hawks-

13

head, Lancashire, group splendidly with the grand mountain scenery.) Dent, West Riding (Pl. 9), and Muker, North Riding, are typical.

In south Devon and parts of west Somerset, many churches are built of the lovely warm-looking red sandstone (Exminster, Devon, and Combe Florey, Somerset), and others in Devon are of slate or granite. The latter is used in many Cornish churches (St Neot). Granite is difficult to carve, but this was certainly managed at the remarkable church of St Mary Magdalen, Launceston.

Kent has a building stone called Kentish rag, much used in that country. It was also easily carried across the Thames and is therefore found in many old south Essex churches.

A type of stone can, of course, vary considerably in colour in different villages. The ironstone of Northamptonshire is deep brown or orange. In that county, a local feature is the use of ironstone and grey oolite freestone together in strips (a good example being the superb tower of Whiston).

The material of the roof covering will, of course, depend upon the locality. Lead may be found anywhere. Red tiles are usual in the South, old grey slates in the South-west and stone tiles in the Cotswolds. Red pantiles are picturesque (Bawburgh, Norfolk, and Holme, Notts), but surely there is no more charming or more homely material than the thatch of the Broads district (Hales, Pl. 21, Filby, Pl. 8, Edingthorpe, Pl. 8, and Potter Heigham, Norfolk, and Fritton, Suffolk).

The height of the exterior roof of the chancel is nearly always lower than that of the nave, but there are occasionally exceptions, which can give an odd appearance (Cotterstock, Northants).

ELEVATION

Local differences, due largely to the building material available as just noted, are far more apparent in elevations than in basic plan. This is understandable as the liturgy which determined the latter was the same in all churches. We will therefore look now at the church as a whole, and what we shall see will depend very much on where we are.

The tower is usually at the west end, but it may be in the middle between nave and chancel, or even occasionally at the side. In East Anglia, if there are aisles, a clerestory with large windows above the aisle roofs is often prominent, and the chancel usually projects eastward clear of the aisle-chapels. At St Mary's, Bury St Edmunds, there are no less than twenty clerestory windows on each side, and at Long Melford, Southwold (Pl. 7) and Blythburgh (Pl. 7), Suffolk, the number is eighteen. Gedney, Lincs, has a beautiful clerestory. See p. 192.

In west Devon and Cornwall, a clerestory is extremely rare, and nave and aisles usually have long low unbroken parallel roofs ending in three gables. Rather curiously this roof arrangement is common in Kent, the other extremity of the country. A clerestory is also rather rare in the extreme south of England. Flat roofs may sometimes be hidden by battlements.

In the East Riding of Yorkshire some churches

are built on as grand a scale as anywhere, but elsewhere in Yorkshire and the North there is often an air of severity, in marked contrast to many homely churches in Sussex and adjoining counties. In the latter area there may only be nave and chancel, both small, with perhaps a turret on top, for often there has been no increase in wealth or population to necessitate enlarging the church since it was built in the Norman or Early English period (Ford, Sussex, Pl. 12). Even if there is an aisle, it may be included with the nave under one long sloping roof.

In other parts of England there is infinite variety. Ground courses, particularly of towers, are often elaborated with projecting mouldings, and sometimes with carving or flush-work (see p. 12).

Large churches and cathedrals sometimes have a crypt beneath them. This does not often apply to small churches, but there are famous Saxon ones at Hexham Priory, Northumberland, Wing, Bucks, and Repton, Derbyshire, and Norman ones at Lastingham, North Riding, Berkswell, Warwickshire, and St Peter-in-the-East, Oxford. Many people know the one at Hythe, Kent, because it is filled with skulls and bones.

A crypt usually raises the chancel, which is, of course, an advantage. The sanctuary at Walpole St Peter, Norfolk (Pl. 42), is splendidly raised because it is built over a footpath.

TOWERS

The old church tower, sometimes with a spire, is the making of the typically English scene. Just think what the countryside would be like if there were no old churches dominating the villages!

We can judge a tower by the arrangement and width of its buttresses (they may be placed diagonally or two at each corner set at right angles, known as rectangular, and a few in Northamptonshire clasp the corners); by the size of the west window (assuming that the tower is at the west end); by the proportions and number of the belfry windows (very important); and by the parapet at the top (whether with pinnacles and battlements).

The grand Perpendicular towers of Somerset in rich stone are unrivalled for composition and exquisite detail. They number about sixty, and occur mostly in groups in particular districts. Shepton Mallet is one of the earliest and from it all the others may be derived. It has three windows abreast in the top stage, but only the centre one is pierced with openings for the sound of the bells, the other windows being blind arcading (blank panelling). (Perforation of belfry windows is a local feature, for elsewhere louvre-boards are usual.) The parapet is straight (without battlements) but pierced with a beautiful pattern. This type is found in the west Mendips at Banwell (Pl. 5), Winscombe, Cheddar, Axbridge, Wedmore, Brent Knoll, Bleadon, Weare and Mark.

Three belfry windows also occur in a group called the east Mendip group, but here all the windows are usually perforated, and the parapet has battlements, as at Ilminster (Pl. 3), Mells, Leigh-on-Mendip (smaller, but one of the most perfect) (Pl. 5)—all of which towers have three windows in the middle stage as well—Bruton, Weston Zoyland and Cranmore. Batcombe is in delightful country and is a beautiful country church. The tower follows the east Mendip type, but lacks pinnacles, which are such a prominent feature of most of these towers: it has a straight parapet, and the belfry windows are prolonged into the stage below. The latter feature, but with two windows, also occurs in the exceptionally fine towers of St Cuthbert's, Wells, Evercreech and Wrington.

Two windows abreast in the top stage, with one in the stage below, and battlemented parapet, are noticeable in a group called the Quantock group. Bishop's Lydeard is one of the earliest, and Huish Episcopi (Pl. 5), adjoining Langport, is one of the most illustrated. Three very similar towers are those of Ile Abbots, Kingston St Mary, and Staple Fitzpaine, and others of the group are at North Petherton, St James's, Taunton, and Kingsbury Episcopi. The pinnacles are extremely beautiful, with slender "flying" pinnacles attached.

The most elaborate tower of all has windows in twos in three stages and exceptionally ornate parapet and pinnacles. It is the tower of St Mary Magdalene's, Taunton.

Certainly one of the most perfect is that of Chewton Mendip, which has two windows in the two upper stories and a most elaborate parapet and pinnacles. Somewhat similar is the tall tower of St John's, Glastonbury. These lace-like parapets and pinnacles are derived from the tower of Gloucester Cathedral. Perhaps, however, the most ornate crown, on an otherwise plain tower, is at Dundry.

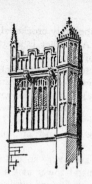

Westwood, Wilts.   Pimperne, Dorset.

Two pinnacles near each corner of the tower but not one on the corner are a characteristic feature of some towers in the south of Somerset, as at Crewkerne (Pl. 7) and Norton-sub-Hamdon, and in Dorset at Milton Abbey and Sherborne Abbey. In the latter county a third pinnacle is usually added at the corner as well, as at Beaminster, Dorchester, Fordington, Charminster and Piddletrenthide (and Hinton St George, Somerset)

The stair turrets of these Somerset towers might terminate in a cap (Bleadon), which in the Bristol area was elongated into a spirelet (Chew Stoke, Somerset, and Pimperne, Dorset); or they might just have their own pinnacles (Crewkerne) (Pl. 7) with sometimes a larger central pinnacle as well (Staple Fitzpaine). As the whole of these lovely towers received most careful treatment, the pinnacles were invariably elaborately crocketed, giving a most pleasing outline. A crocket is a projecting crook-like leaf or bunch of leaves.

We can only recommend a visit to Somerset, so that all these splendid towers can be examined in detail (see back endpaper). Outside Somerset and Dorset there are only two towers that reach the same high standard. They are at Probus, Cornwall, and Chittlehampton, Devon, and are obviously influenced by Somerset.

Of towers outside that area, very special mention must be made of the central tower at Canterbury Cathedral, Magdalen Tower, Oxford (and the tower of Merton College as well), and among parish churches, Titchmarsh, Northants, St Neots, Hunts, and Gresford, Denbigh.

The next best tower area is the East Riding of Yorkshire. For sheer size the Perpendicular towers are unrivalled. Pride of place is taken by Beverley Minster (Pl. 9), where the two west towers are of perfect proportions and are easily the most successful west towers in the whole country. (A minster now means a church that was not connected with a monastery.) We then have Hedon, Holy Trinity, Hull, Howden, Cottingham and St Mary's, Beverley (Pl. 9). They are all central towers and are masterpieces. Great Driffield is noble.

Some Yorkshire towers are capped with lace-like forms of open-work parapet (Tickhill, West Riding). Small towers usually have small pinnacles.

In Worcestershire, Gloucestershire and Wiltshire some of the larger fifteenth-century towers are ornamented with panelling (Great Malvern Priory

20

and Evesham, Worcs, Chipping Campden, Glos, and Westwood, Wilts).

An octagonal storey on top of a tower makes a striking picture. There are three notable examples: Lowick (Pl. 10) and Fotheringhay, Northants, and Boston, Lincs, the latter being the highest tower, 288 feet.

West Devon and Cornwall have some tall fifteenth-century towers, often of great blocks of granite, with large octagonal pinnacles having crocketed spirelets (St Cleer, St Erme and Poughill, Pl. 6, Cornwall, and Widecombe, Devon). The smaller towers usually have pinnacles, but of rather crude construction; they are, however, an unmistakable part of the glorious West Country scene (St Levan, Cornwall, Pl. 6, and Hennock, Devon). Some towers in Devon taper towards the top (Stoke Gabriel). A local feature in south Devon is that the stair turret is often in the middle of one of the sides of the tower instead of at the corner (Ipplepen and Ashburton, Pl. 6).

In East Anglia flint is the material, as mentioned. The Perpendicular towers are usually tall, and on the coast are very tall as landmarks for shipping (Brightlingsea, Essex, Southwold, Pl. 7, Walberswick, Covehithe and Kessingland, Suffolk, and Winterton, Happisburgh, Cromer and Blakeney, Norfolk). The buttresses often stop at the bottom of the belfry stage which gives these towers their pleasing outline (Filby, Norfolk, Pl. 8). In the middle stage a square aperture filled with elaborate tracery is called a Norfolk air-hole. Battlements sometimes take a stepped form (Walcott and Filby,

21

Pl. 8, Norfolk). Many towers, however, end in a straight parapet and are probably unfinished (Trunch, Norfolk, and Southwold, Suffolk, Pl. 7); this nevertheless entirely suits Norfolk, for a flat parapet harmonizes with flat country, but it would be quite out of place in Devon. It is possible that battlements and pinnacles or even a spire were intended, but to import the necessary stone was costly and money may already have run out. Where pinnacles do occur, quite often they take the form of figures or animals (Filby, Pl. 8, Honingham, Blofield and Acle, Norfolk). The stairway is often internal, but even if there is a turret it is rarely prominent, and it nearly always ends below the top.

Great towers (away from the coast) can be seen at Redenhall, Cawston, Sall and Wymondham Abbey, Norfolk, and at Lavenham, Bungay, Eye, Stoke-by-Nayland and Woodbridge, Suffolk. The average tower in Norfolk is well above the average anywhere else, both in height and in appearance. We mention Reedham, Brisley, Great Massingham, Grimston, Hindringham, Northrepps and Southrepps. Yet even here, as everywhere else in England, it is the innumerable small, simple, unassuming towers that possess an unsurpassed charm, as, for instance, Burgh-next-Aylsham, Norfolk, and Framsden (Pl. 1), Suffolk. There are, indeed, over one thousand old church towers in Norfolk and Suffolk.

It is sometimes said that the round towers of Norfolk and Suffolk obviated the necessity of obtaining stone for buttresses; but a square tower can be built without dressed stone, as at Beeston Regis, Norfolk. The better opinion is that they were built

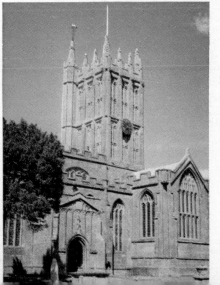

Plate 3

top Beeston Regis, on the Norfolk coast. Fine pre-Reformation screen panels of the Apostles.

left Ilminster, Somerset, a grand Perpendicular tower.

Plate 4 *above* Aldermaston, Berks, the Annunciation in the gorgeous colours of 13th-century glass

below Bisham, Berks, on the River Thames, the sumptuous monument to Lady Hoby and her family, 1609.

Forncett St Peter, Norfolk.   Wotton, Surrey.

for strength and for defensive purposes—either as a
look-out or to accommodate the villagers if there
was an attack by the Danes. They are all near the
sea or a river, are Saxon in origin, and originally
they never had any opening low down, access being
gained to the upper part by a ladder hauled up
afterwards. Haddiscoe, Norfolk, is one of the finest
and still has its Saxon belfry windows, as has
Forncett St Peter, Norfolk. Gissing, Hales (Pl. 21)
and Runhall (Pl. 8), Norfolk, are typical. Sometimes
a later octagonal upper storey has been added (Potter
Heigham and Edingthorpe, Pl. 8, Norfolk). There
are 112 round towers in Norfolk, 41 in Suffolk, six
in Essex and only seven elsewhere.

Similarly many towers on the Welsh and Scottish
borders were built for defence against the then
unpleasant inhabitants of those countries. Bosbury,

Herefords, Bedale, North Riding, Ormside, Westmorland, and Great Salkeld, Cumberland, are typical.

The old brick towers of Essex with their warm-looking colouring are as delightful as can be found anywhere. Splendid examples can be seen at Gestingthorpe, Ingatestone, Rochford, Great Holland, Wickham St Paul and Castle Hedingham in that county and at St Mary-at-Elms in Ipswich.

Kent has a most distinctive type of Perpendicular tower. There is a prominent octagonal stair turret at the corner projecting above the tower and there are no pinnacles (Seal, Pl. 8, and Charing). Belfry windows in Kent are usually square-headed. This type of tower (and it is very pleasing) is also found here and there in the south Midlands (Husborne Crawley, Beds), and in the West Country. Such towers in the latter area may have pinnacles (Bradninch, Devon), and the turret may be square (sometimes with its own four pinnacles, as at Affpuddle, Dorset, and Gwinear, Cornwall). Often the turret is not quite at the corner. (The last feature is also found in a small group in Suffolk, as at Monks Eleigh.)

Occasionally a tower is octagonal (Sancton, East Riding), and there are several in Somerset (North Curry). (The whole of this church has pierced parapets—a pleasing local feature.)

A pyramidal cap (p. 34) within the parapet can be found (Bradenham and Leckhampstead, Bucks), but a small version is common in Sussex (Seaford).

Some towers in the Thames and Waveney Valleys have octagonal buttresses (Henley, Oxon, and Eye,

Gwinear, Cornwall.   Bradenham, Bucks.
            North Curry, Somerset.

Suffolk; Magdalen Tower, Oxford, is the most superb example).

A local characteristic of the Welsh Border Country is a belfry with a pyramidal roof placed upon a pyramidal roof surmounting the tower; a rare example near London is at Wotton, Surrey.

In the north-west Midlands the whole tower is occasionally constructed of the local black-and-white timber and plaster (Pirton and Warndon, Worcs).

Around Stamford, Lincs, are some distinctive fifteenth-century towers with prominent parapet, pinnacles and belfry windows, the head of such windows being bisected by the centre mullion, a curious local feature. Great Ponton, Lincs, is a fine example.

In the east Midlands the finer Perpendicular towers developed exceedingly fine and well-proportioned belfry windows which were used sometimes in pairs as double windows and sometimes singly. Above them was almost invariably a band of

25

ornament (a most satisfying addition) and then battlements and possibly pinnacles. Examples are at Great Staughton and Hamerton, Hunts, Stockerston, Leics, Belton, Rutland, and Warkton and Whiston, Northants, the last being particularly elaborate.

In the north Midlands some towers may have double belfry windows under a single ogee hood-mould as at Haselbech, Northants (Pl. 10).

If a village could not afford to rebuild the whole of its tower in the Perpendicular period and yet wanted the latest fashion, then just the belfry storey in that style would be added to an earlier lower storey, possibly in a different type of stone; Moulton and Ecton, Northants, are examples. At Little Houghton, Northants, the lower portion of the tower is Early English with fine arcading of that period, and the belfry storey is a splendid Perpendicular addition. The tower of Ketton, Rutland, and the lower part of the tower of Melton Mowbray, Leics (Pl. 10), are excellent specimens of Early English work; the former is surmounted by an Early English broach spire and the latter by a notable Perpendicular belfry storey—one can therefore make one's choice between the two.

A simple church tower of medieval date is usually satisfying, with battlements only (Stanton Harcourt, Oxon, and Chirton, Wilts) or with four pinnacles (Upper Slaughter, Glos), but eight pinnacles are, however, very effective (Averham and Rolleston, Notts, Hook Norton and Great Rollright, Oxon, and Badsey, Worcs).

Some churches, particularly in East Anglia, have a spirelet bell-fleche on top of the tower (East Harling,

Ketton,   Burwell,   Ickford,
Rutland.   Cambs.   Bucks.

Norfolk, and Burwell, Cambs); after the Reformation the fleche was usually a cupola (dome-shaped), as at Wivenhoe and Tilty, Essex, and several west Middlesex churches. The bell-fleche may be on top of the stair turret, as at Cheshunt, Herts.

Gabled or saddle-back towers occur mostly in poorer districts of the stone area and often indicate that the tower is unfinished. Such a tower does, however, harmonize with the village scene, as at Duntisbourne Abbots and Bagendon in the Cotswolds. An example of a tower that was obviously intended to take a gabled form is at Ickford, Bucks.

Cartmel Priory, Lancs, has a unique tower; it consists of a square tower set diagonally on a larger square below.

Quite frequently a triangular mark is seen on the east side of a tower; this is the ridge mark of the earlier more steeply pitched roof of the nave.

27

If there is no stone staircase up a tower, it would probably be ascended by a wooden ladder. The original wooden stairway still remains in the Norman tower of Brabourne, Kent. It is an amazing sight and is a good example of the interest often tucked away in unknown places. The oak steps are over 800 years old and the huge timbers were obviously cut from a very ancient tree—so just calculate when that tree must have been planted!

If is often difficult to reach the top of a tower, but effort will be rewarded. A lovely view of the countryside is generally obtained, and everything seems to look better from a height.

Detached Towers

Sometimes a tower is detached. It is usually in marshy country, where the tower could not be built in its usual position. West Walton, Norfolk (Pl. 11), in the Fens, has a notable Early English example, and Beccles, Suffolk, on the River Waveney, has a huge one of the Perpendicular period, but better known are the timber spire at Brookland, Kent (Pl. 13), on Romney Marsh, and the bell-cage at East Bergholt, Suffolk (Pl. 12).

Towers of the different Building Periods

The finest and most numerous towers are of the Perpendicular period, as we have shown, but towers of all periods can be found almost anywhere, and they can, of course, be dated by their details. A fine tower of the Decorated period is at Whissendine, Rutland, and there is an elaborate example (with a stone spire) at Heckington, Lincs. Early English towers can be well studied at West Walton, Norfolk

(Pl. 11), Bury, Hunts, Brackley, Northants, and Haddenham, Bucks. (Often, however, the finest Early English towers have stone broach spires.) Magnificent Norman towers are to be found at Tewkesbury Abbey, Glos, Castor, Northants (Pl. 11), St Albans Cathedral and St Clement's, Sandwich, Kent, but smaller examples are equally pleasing, as at East Meon, Hants, Old Shoreham, Sussex, South Lopham, Norfolk, Iffley, Oxon, and Stewkley, Bucks. The usual arrangement of belfry windows is two round-headed arches divided by a shaft and recessed within a large round-headed containing arch. A circular opening is also quite usual.

In the Saxon period the belfry windows were never recessed. They usually consist of round-headed openings divided by a mid-wall shaft baluster-shaped (p. 23). An easy feature to detect is long-and-short work at the corners of the tower, the corner stones being alternately horizontal and vertical. Sometimes

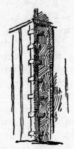

Saxon long-and-short work.
Earls Barton, Northants.

the surface of a tower is covered with pilaster strips, obviously copied from ornamental work on the wooden buildings of the time. These last two features are usually late Saxon work.

Lincolnshire has a number of Saxon towers, but the one most illustrated is Earls Barton, Northants (Pl. 10). St Peter's, Barton-on-Humber, Lincs, is somewhat similar, and there are examples at Bywell St Andrew and Ovingham, Northumberland, Appleton-le-Street, North Riding, Barnack, Northants, and at Oxford (St Michael's) and Cambridge (St Benet's). Most of the East Anglian round towers are Saxon. The tower of Sompting, near Worthing, Sussex, is well known, but its gabled top is unique, although the type is common in the Rhineland.

Towers of the seventeenth and eighteenth centuries have large round-headed windows, often with projecting keystones, a classical balustrade with urns instead of pinnacles, and possibly a cupola (Wimborne St Giles, Dorset) (Pl. 11). The fine tower of St Mary's, Warwick, 1704, is Perpendicular in outline, but with Classical details. We are not really concerned here with Victorian churches, but we mention three towers which do enhance the countryside—Orlingbury, Northants, and Northaw, Herts, and Cattistock, Dorset.

If there is no tower or timber turret, then a bell or two may be hung in an open bell-cote—as at Kelmscott, Oxon, and Little Casterton and Essendine, Rutland—or, more rarely, in a bell-cage, as at Brympton D'Evercy, Somerset. These were, of course, generally in poorer districts unable to afford anything more.

Saxon.
Sompting, Sussex.

Essendine,
Rutland.

Figure Sculpture on Towers

Many of the fine Somerset towers have numerous niches for figures, and often the original figures still remain, as at Ile Abbots. The figure of Our Lord surrounded by angels may be seen at Chewton Mendip and Batcombe. At Minehead there are representations of the Holy Trinity and St Michael, whilst at Hartland, Devon, there is a large figure of the patron saint, St Nectan. At Fairford, Glos, are quaint figures, and at Clanfield, Oxon, St Stephen holds his stones and a book on the tower of the church dedicated to him.

Gargoyles are referred to later (p. 68).

BELLS

A tower was built to contain bells, and it is amazing that over 3,000 medieval ones are still hanging and ringing in belfries. Such bells were often dedicated to a saint and they might have a prayer or inscription inscribed in beautiful lettering. Initial letters in the form of crosses, word stops, lettering and foundry marks are of great interest and beauty, and yet are rarely seen as few people climb to the belfry.

In England medieval bells are not usually dated, the earliest one with a date being at Claughton, Lancs, 1296. Older bells do, however, remain at Caversfield and Goring, Oxon. The earliest bells were long and narrow. After the Reformation, inscriptions, usually in English, were often rhymes of a somewhat secular nature and incorporated the name of the founder.

The richest counties for the study of old bells are Norfolk, Suffolk, Devon and Somerset.

Change-ringing was introduced in the middle of the seventeenth century. It is unknown outside England. The bells are rung one after the other, the order changing each time, as in the complicated methods known as Grandsire, Treble Bob and so on. On eight bells 40,320 changes are possible. About 1,600 changes can be rung in an hour and it is rare to have more than five or six thousand rung at one time. To ring all the changes possible on eight bells without stopping would therefore take about 24 hours.

Many churches now have a ring of eight bells

and even more have six. There are at present about 5,200 churches in England with rings of five or more bells. The greatest numbers are in Devon, followed by Somerset. Rings of bells are almost exclusively confined to the Church of England.

The essential feature of ringing in a peal is that the bell should perform an almost complete revolution each time the rope is pulled, starting from an inverted position. A stay on the headstock attached to a wheel is stopped by a slider which prevents the bell from performing a complete revolution.

The bells are rung from the ringing-chamber which is usually midway up the tower. Sometimes, however, they are rung from the ground, and when the tower is central, as at Somerby, Leics, and Hemingborough, East Riding (Pl. 15), the ringers are in full view of the congregation. When this arrangement applies to a tower the base of which forms the entrance to the church, the congregation have to pass round the circle of ringers. Crowland Abbey, Lincs, is an example.

Ringers' rhymes on boards (St Endellion, Cornwall) are usually quaint and may date from the seventeenth or eighteenth century; there is always a fine for wearing a hat or spur.

The bells ring out with messages of hope, joy and worship. Surely there is no sweeter or more melodious sound, in this age of noise, than that of church bells echoing over the countryside.

The illustration (Pl. 12) shows the interior of the quaint detached bell-cage on ground level at East Bergholt, Suffolk. (For the Sanctus bell, see p. 157.)

TIMBER BELFRIES AND SPIRES

Spires may be of timber or stone according to the locality. No doubt the earliest form of covering of a tower was a low pyramidal cap, as at Old Shoreham and Jevington, Sussex; this was soon heightened as at Yapton, Sussex, and Limpsfield, Surrey, and this again soon became elongated into an octagonal spire. These low caps may be covered with timber, red tiles, lead, copper, stone tiles, or grey slates according to the district.

| Jevington, | Yapton, | Crowhurst, |
| Sussex. | Sussex. | Surrey. |

In the south-east of England, where timber is plentiful, small timber belfries were often placed on the roof of the nave at its west end, and these belfries had either a small cap (as at Ford, Pl. 12, and Tortington in Sussex where belfry and cap are painted white) or a spire, usually covered with wooden shingles, which might be either of moderate height, as at Alfold, Surrey, Birdbrook, Essex, and Brenzett, Kent (Pl. 12), or tall and slender as at Crowhurst, Surrey, and Cowden, Kent. These belfries are supported inside the church on a massive timber framework. In Essex the whole of some remarkable towers which support a timber belfry or spire are themselves of timber, as at West Hanningfield, Margaretting, Magdalen Laver, Greensted (Pl. 13), Stock, Blackmore and Navestock.

In Surrey and Sussex a large spire of timber shingles overlapping a tower is very common, and the spire may be massive, as at Compton, Surrey, Bury, Sussex, and Bapchild (Pl. 13) and Patrixbourne, Kent, squat (Old Romney, Kent) (Pl. 13), or more slender, as at Playden and Horsted Keynes, Sussex, and Hever and Eynsford (Pl. 14), Kent.

Timber spires overlapping the tower are usually chamfered, which means that the square base of the spire changes to octagonal form by the four corners being cut away or chamfered. (This chamfer actually covers the two posts from each corner which support the collar upon which the spire is constructed.) Occasionally, however, such spires are of a type known as broach spires (which have only one post from each corner to the collar and which are covered by broaches or sloping pyramids). As with stone spires, timber-framed spires may sometimes rise from within the parapet of the tower (Great Burstead, Essex). See front endpaper.

Sometimes a timber-framed spire was covered with lead, which gives a whitish appearance. Examples *overlapping the tower*: Long Sutton, Lincs (the oldest), East Meon, Hants, Barnstaple, Swimbridge and Braunton (Pl. 14), Devon, Ickleton, Cambs, Hadleigh, Suffolk, and Godalming, Surrey

Hitchin,
Herts.

St Margaret,
Lothbury, City.

Shipton,
Salop.

(some with an outside bell); *within the tower parapet*: Hemel Hempstead, Herts, Great Baddow, Essex (Pl. 14), and Ash-next-Sandwich, Kent: and *on a timber belfry*; Stanford Rivers, Essex (Pl. 12). No doubt the best known is the crooked spire of lead at Chesterfield, Derbyshire. If a green spire is seen, the covering would be of copper (Wingham, Kent, within the parapet, Barham, near by, overlapping the parapet, and Chigwell, Essex, on a timber belfry).

A needle spire, usually of lead, is popular in Hertfordshire, hence the name Herts spike (Flamstead, Hitchin, Little Munden, Great Munden and Little Hadham). Rather curiously a favourite feature of churches built today is the needle spire (Coventry Cathedral), which is characteristic of this Space Age.

Some towers of stone might have been unfinished, or the upper part might since have disappeared, and the termination may now be a timber turret with possibly a pyramidal cap, as at Shipton, Salop.

STONE SPIRES

The earliest stone spire may be at Barnack, Northants, but the earliest group is a type found around Oxford, all of the early thirteenth century. There are four characteristics:

(a) the spire overlaps the tower;
(b) there are tall massive pinnacles at the corners;
(c) there are no spire-lights;
(d) there are large dormer windows at the base of the spire on the four cardinal sides. Examples are at Oxford Cathedral, Witney, Bampton (Pl. 14), Broadwell and Shipton-under-Wychwood.

Broach Spires

In the same century the broach spire was evolved and this type is found only in England. The square tower changes to an octagonal spire by means of broaches at the corners, which are really just a covering for the arches inside the tower at its angles which support the diagonal sides of the spire (see front endpaper). Broaches vary considerably in size, from large and steep pitch to low and insignificant. This type almost always overlaps the tower; there are no pinnacles, and instead of dormer windows there are two or more tiers of spire-lights. These may occur on the cardinal sides only or on the diagonal sides also, when they are usually in alternate rows.

The object of spire-lights is to afford ventilation, to light the interior of the spire, and, of course, decoration; to allow the wind to pass through a spire did not necessarily reduce wind pressure. In late spires, if employed at all, spire-lights are few and small.

The broach spire is nearly always thirteenth or sometimes fourteenth century, although occasionally used in the Perpendicular period, as at Irchester, Northants. In most cases tower and spire form one admirable unit. Amongst so many in Northamptonshire, south Lincolnshire and surrounding districts, it is difficult to choose a few of special note, but mention must be made of Aldwincle St Peter (Pl. 15), Polebrook, Raunds and Warmington, Northants, St Mary's, Stamford, Ewerby, Frampton, North Rauceby, Aunsby and Threekingham, Lincs, Keyston, Warboys and Buckworth, Hunts, Newark, Notts, Market Harborough, Leics, and Ketton (p. 27) and Barrowden, Rutland.

As with towers, so with spires. The small unpretentious ones are often as lovely as any and fit in perfectly with the village scene.

The county of Huntingdon is very rural and tourists seem to keep to the Great North Road and therefore miss it; yet it has a wealth of fine archi-

tecture. Four neighbouring villages on the Hunting-
don-Thrapston road have small but perfect broach
spires, the towers themselves having the well-
proportioned belfry windows of the area and usually
a band of ornament at the top. (This latter indicates a late date and it superseded the corbel-table
or row of small projecting ornament used earlier.)
The villages are Ellington, Easton, Spaldwick and
Brington. Broughton in the same county is typical.

Sometimes the broach spire is stumpy, as at
Holme, Notts, but it is nevertheless extremely
picturesque. On the other hand a broach spire can
occasionally be long and slender, as at Shurdington
and Leckhampton, Glos. The chamfer type, so
common in timber spires, is very rare in stone spires,
but can be seen at Denford and Etton, Northants,
Bythorn, Hunts, and Seaton, Rutland.

Outside the stone spire area, old stone spires are
rare or quite unknown (e.g. in Kent). Devon and
Cornwall, rather curiously, have a few, all of the
simplest design. In the south of Cornwall are
two broach spires which are almost identical and
are of the crudest possible type: Rame, high up on
its headland with the sea on three sides and exposed
to rain and every wind that blows; and Sheviock
in an adjoining parish, but completely sheltered in
a beautiful combe; St Enodoc on its golf course
opposite Padstow is also similar.

Parapet Spires

These spires do not overlap the tower, but rise
from within the parapet. They are usually of the
fourteenth or fifteenth centuries. The advantage

of this type is that a ladder and scaffolding can be placed on the tower if repairs are needed instead of erecting them from the ground, as is, of course, necessary with the earlier broach spires, and one can walk round the base of the spire.

Abroad it is often impossible to tell where the tower finishes and the spire commences, but in England there is nearly always a distinct line of demarcation between the two, and the parapet type certainly assists in this respect.

The most superb parish church spire is at Louth, Lincs. It is early sixteenth century and is 294 feet high, dominating the green valley between the Wolds and the Marsh. The tower itself is a grand one, and from its four crocketed pinnacles (no less than 52 feet high) four most effective flying buttresses jump across to the spire.

The spire itself has crockets, a feature of late spires. Crockets form steps for steeplejacks. Long lines tend to seem hollow in the middle and so a slight bulge (or entasis) was often given to a spire midway. The genius who designed this spire obtained this result by increasing the size of the crockets about one-third of the way up. Tower and spire are of equal height, as they should be. (At Hemingborough, East Riding, Pl. 15, and Glinton, Northants, the height of the spire greatly exceeds that of the tower.)

Moulton, Lincs (Pl. 15), is another lovely example with most effective flying buttresses. These are not always satisfactory: at the noble church of Patrington, East Riding, with a fine spire, they seem to be of little practical assistance.

The parapet type of spire is more common than the broach type and occurs frequently in the stone spire areas mentioned, particularly in south Lincolnshire, where it is possible to see at one glance at least a dozen soaring upwards—each one noble. Spires were particularly favoured in the fourteenth century, and spires are common in south Lincolnshire as many churches in that area are of that period. The splendid church of Heckington, with its elaborate Flowing tracery, is specially worthy of mention. Great parapet spires can be seen at Grantham, Lincs, Higham Ferrers, Rushden, Kettering and Oundle, Northants, and Whittlesey, Cambs. It is, however, in innumerable villages once again that smaller, but no less perfect, examples are to be found. The following are all lovely, but will be quite unknown: Claypole, Gosberton, Donington, Helpringham, Billingborough, Brant Broughton, Silk Willoughby, Quadring and Surfleet (the last two with leaning towers), Lincs, Easton Maudit, Bulwick and Wakerley, Northants, Yaxley and Great Gidding, Hunts, South Luffenham, Rutland, Queniborough, Leics, Eltisley, Cambs (Pl. 16), and Hanslope, Bucks. A really charming diminutive parapet spire is at Weekley, Northants (Pl. 15), where the church makes a fitting end to the picturesque village street.

There is also a small group of stone spires treated rather differently from those mentioned above, having an arrangement of double pinnacles, one above the other. Five superb examples are Salisbury Cathedral (the highest, 404 feet), St Mary's, Oxford, King's Sutton, Northants, Laughtonen-le-Morthen, West Riding, and Ruardean, Glos.

Another small group, but very effective, has a spire rising from an octagonal storey surmounting the tower, as at Wilby (Pl. 16) and Nassington, Northants, Exton, Rutland, and All Saints', North Street, York.

Only three churches in England possess a tower and another tower with a spire: Purton and Wanborough, Wilts, and Ormskirk, Lancs.

The earliest of the great towers of Somerset, Shepton Mallet, was designed for a spire, and the lower courses were indeed built, but the tower looked so well without a spire that it was apparently thought better to leave well alone. Yatton in the same county has an incomplete spire, and a truncated timber one is familiar to visitors to Porlock. Perpendicular church towers did not therefore generally have a spire.

A small spire poised on elegant flying buttresses rising up from the corners of a tower was a novel idea. Newcastle Cathedral is an example and there is another at Faversham, Kent.

Sir Christopher Wren used the design at St Dunstan-in-the-East (Great Tower Street), and in none of his spires did he express greater confidence. We must therefore now have a word on

Wren's Towers and Spires

The square mile of the Roman and medieval City of London had about a hundred churches at the Reformation; St Andrew Undershaft (Leadenhall Street) is typical of that period. The majority were destroyed in the Great Fire, 1666, and Wren then rebuilt fifty-one, mostly of Portland stone. Some of these have since been demolished or wrecked in the blitz, but the City still possesses some forty churches, and some towers on their own.

Wren's real genius is shown in his towers and spires. The stone spire of St Mary-le-Bow, Cheapside, is both wonderful and perfect, and every detail is worth careful study. Other elegant spires of stone are at St Bride's, Fleet Street, and St Vedast's, Foster Lane (Pl. 11). Three towers are surmounted by elaborate stone turrets or structures, somewhat similar and yet differing in detail: St Michael's, Paternoster Royal, St James's, Garlickhithe, and St Stephen's, Walbrook.

It is, however, in his lead turrets and spires that the greatest variety is found. The following are all exceptionally pleasing: St Magnus, London Bridge, St Margaret's, Lothbury, St Martin's, Ludgate (acting as a foil to the dome of St Paul's), St Edmund's, Lombard Street, St Mary Abchurch (near Cannon Street), St Peter's, Cornhill (now copper), and St Benet's, Upper Thames Street.

For an interior, much as Wren would have left it, one cannot do better than visit St Mary-at-Hill, Eastcheap, and St Mary Abchurch.

WEATHER-VANES

On top of the tower or spire may be a weather-vane. It is often a cock for vigilance (Oakham, Rutland, has one of the oldest), but it may sometimes be the emblem of the patron saint. A very large cock at Knapton, Norfolk, is combined with keys and sword for Saints Peter and Paul.

A large key for St Peter is above the churches dedicated to him in Cornhill, City of London, and at Bedford and Brackley, Northants. At several churches, however, a key vane does not indicate that dedication, as at St Botolph's, Aspley Guise, Beds. The gridiron of St Lawrence surmounts his

Weather-vane.
Knapton, Norfolk.

Battlements.
Wisbech, Cambs.

churches at St Lawrence, Jewry, City of London, Ramsgate, Kent, Tidmarsh, Berks, and in Essex at Upminster, Elmstead and Bradfield.

A dragon is quite a favourite. At St Mary-le-Bow, Cheapside, City of London, he is 8 feet 10 inches in length, weighs 2 cwt. and is poised 230 feet up. Similar monsters can be seen at Ottery St Mary, Devon, Sittingbourne, Kent, and Upton, Norfolk.

A fish (p. 190) is also popular, as at Filey and Flamborough, East Riding, and St John the Baptist's, Southover, Lewes, and Piddinghoe, Sussex. A ship is not uncommon. It even has red sails at Tollesbury, Essex. At East Dereham, Norfolk, where there is a large detached tower in addition to the central tower of the church, the vane is a deer (a pun).

44

Vanes are often dated and may be heraldic (Etchingham, Sussex). Many, however, are most unusual, and a fascinating pastime is to spot and record them—for instance, on the fine tower of Great Ponton, Lincs, is a violin.

Two of interest of recent date come to mind: St Martin and the beggar at Chipping Ongar, Essex, and a plough with E 11 R at Northrepps, Norfolk.

Weathercocks certainly have a very early origin, for one appears in the Bayeux Tapestry of the eleventh century. The Englishman has always been interested in the direction of the wind, so what is more natural than to place a vane on top of the highest building in the village?

CLOCKS AND CLOCK-JACKS

Most churches would have had clocks in medieval days, but it would probably be as late as the seventeenth century before the simple clocks of village churches had dials.

The hour and its quarters were often struck on the bell or bells by jacks, figures which were ingeniously devised and brightly coloured. A delightful trio of such figures still hard at work can be seen at Exeter St Mary Steps (Pl. 16). On the clock dial a circle of numerals indicates the hours. Within the circle the dial rotates, and on it are fixed the sun and five stars, the sun pointing the hour. One end of the minute hand is tipped with the crescent moon. The quarter jacks hold a pike in one hand and in the other a hammer with which they strike the bell under the little platform on which each stands. The central figure has a rigid rod in his hands, but he nods his head at each stroke of the hour.

Other jacks still working can be seen at Rye, Sussex (the great pendulum swinging free in the body of the church), Wimborne Minster, Dorset, St Thomas's, Salisbury, and All Saints', Leicester. Tall single jacks which have retired, as they are not in their original positions, remain at Southwold (fifteenth century) and Blythburgh, Suffolk, and Minehead, Somerset. The best known and most notable medieval clock is, of course, in Wells Cathedral. Ottery St Mary, Devon, also has a medieval clock.

Elaborate projecting clocks became popular in the seventeenth century, and Wren often combined them very charmingly with his towers (St Mary-le-Bow, Cheapside, and St Magnus, London Bridge). At West Acre, Norfolk, instead of figures on the dial are the words "Watch and pray" (not prey)— very good advice, but one wonders if any connection is meant between a watch and a clock!

PORCHES

After the tower, the porch is usually the most prominent projection on the exterior of the church. It had its liturgical uses and therefore great care was bestowed upon it.

In medieval times at a baptism the priest received the sponsors with the infant in the porch, began the service there, and then led the way into the church for the remainder of the rite. The first parts of the services of Churching of Women and of Marriage were also conducted in the porch. It was important in the great procession on Palm Sunday, with perhaps a temporary gallery for singers from which palm branches were strewn in the way. (Remains of such a gallery can be seen at Weston-in-Gordano, Somerset.) The New Fire was certainly kindled and blessed in the porch on Holy Saturday.

The Church always offered sanctuary to an offender until a trial could be arranged, and the porch would be the part first reached by him (or her). The handle of a church door is, in fact, often referred to as a sanctuary knocker.

Many porches have an upper storey with a room. This would have been the local strong-room. A custodian may even have lived there, and there would then no doubt have been a window through to the church. Later the room may have been used as an armoury—pieces of armour, particularly helmets, often remain in a church. (The most complete armoury is at Mendlesham, Suffolk.) The room may also have been used to house a library and later still as a lumber room. Some, however, have now been very effectively converted into small chapels.

A niche, usually on the right-hand side near the church entrance, would be a stoup. Sometimes it is supported on a shaft. An exceptionally elaborate one is in the small and isolated church of Caldecote, Herts. The stoup holds holy water—water that has been blessed by a priest. The devout worshipper on entering and leaving the church reverently dips the fingers of his right hand in the water and makes the sign of the cross to indicate self-consecration and a renewal of baptismal vows.

The material of the porch, like all parts of the church, as we have seen, will vary according to the geological strata. Where stone is plentiful, porches will, of course, be on a noble scale. At Cirencester, Glos, is the largest porch and it was indeed the Town Hall. Not far away, at another wool centre, Northleach, Glos (Pl. 16), is perhaps the finest porch of all, beautifully adorned with turrets, pinnacles and niches (containing original figures of the Holy Trinity and the Virgin and Child). East Anglia has some splendid examples, often with flush-work (p. 12, Kersey and Framsden, Pl. 1, Suffolk), and generally sat upon by animals or figures (Mendlesham Suffolk). Pulham St Mary the Virgin, Norfolk (Pl. 17), and Woolpit and Beccles, Suffolk, are notable.

At Addlethorpe, Lincs, is a beautiful porch with its original gable cross carved with the crucifixion and the Virgin and Child. All these porches are of the fifteenth century.

A fine example of the fourteenth century is at Heckington, Lincs (Pl. 19). Thirteenth-century porches were usually only of slight projection, as at Skelton, near York, North Riding, and West Walton, Norfolk (Pl. 18). The Norman porch at Malmesbury Abbey, Wilts, has truly magnificent doorways and carvings of the apostles (Pl. 17).

In the south-east of England, the plentiful supply of timber gives us a number of porches of that material dating back to the fourteenth or fifteenth centuries. The gabled portion in front (called a barge-board) and the side openings were usually skilfully carved, and the entrance arch was constructed of great tree trunks. High Halden, Kent, West Grinstead, Sussex, Margaretting, Essex, and West Challow and Long Wittenham, Berks, are just a few among many, but perhaps the finest is at Boxford, Suffolk (Pl. 17), of the fourteenth century. An example of black-and-white, or half-timber and plaster, is at Berkswell, Warwickshire. Porches of brick have been mentioned (p. 13).

Saxon doorway.
Barnack, Northants.

Stoup.
Caldecote, Herts.

Cornwall has its own type built of blocks of granite (St Neot).

A famous Renaissance porch is at St Mary's, Oxford.

The roof of the porch may be vaulted, particularly in stone areas. The bosses at the intersection of the ribs should be carefully noted, as it is much easier to see them than those high up on the roof of the church. At Cley, Norfolk, is a boss of a boy with trousers down, being caned.

The porch may also, of course, retain its old wooden roof (Kersey, Suffolk), again often with interesting bosses of that material: at Landkey, Devon, is one showing four stags, but there is only one head. The wagon roof of the West Country is particularly charming in this position (Laneast, Cornwall).

DOORWAYS
(and ornament)

(Reference should also be made to the section on Piers and Arches)

These differ according to their date. The main characteristics are:

Saxon High and narrow with round arch; there are no recessed orders (or sub-arches); and large square impost stones (the horizontal support from which an arch springs) are prominent (Barnack, Northants). Sometimes the head is triangular.

Norman The round arch continues, but there are now usually a number of recessed arches, and under each arch, at the sides, are small shafts.

The arches are often highly ornamented, the favourite ornaments being chevron or zigzag, pellet, billet, cable, diamond, lozenge, nailhead (usually late), star, double cone and beak-head.

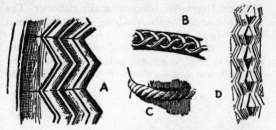

A. Chevron or Zigzag.   B and C. Cable.
D. Lozenge.

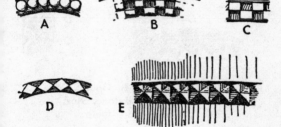

A. Pellet.   B and C. Billet.
D. Diamond.   E. Nailhead.

Norman ornament.

Iffley (Pl. 18) and Barford St Michael, Oxon,
Tutbury, Staffs, Windrush, Glos, Heckingham,
Norfolk (Pl. 18), Adel, Wighill and Fishlake, West
Riding, Stillingfleet and Kirkburn, East Riding, and
Alne, North Riding, are among the finest, and

Kilpeck, Herefords, is exceptionally elaborate. The doorways at Malmesbury Abbey, Wilts, have been mentioned (p. 48).

Above the head of the doorway, but within the containing arch, is a space called a tympanum, and this also was often elaborately carved. There are

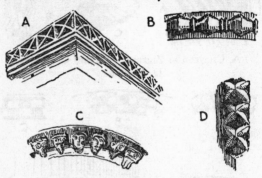

A. Star. B. Double Cone
C. Beak-heads, Elkstone, Glos.
D. 13th-century dog-tooth.

many examples in the Cotswolds, as at Elkstone (with Christ in Majesty and the symbols of the Evangelists) and Quenington (which has two remarkable ones, the one illustrated, Pl. 18, showing the Harrowing of Hell or the releasing of souls by Christ); also at Siddington and Moreton Valence (all in Glos). Herefordshire has several, as at Brinsop, Rowlstone and Stretton Sugwas; others are at Handborough, Oxon, Dinton, Bucks, Barfreston and Patrixbourne, Kent. Aston Eyre, Salop, has a life-like carving of the Entry into Jerusalem (Pl. 17).

Early English The pointed arch is introduced and continues throughout the medieval period. The arch is usually acute and the mouldings are deeply cut. At the sides may be one or two detached shafts and the capitals might have the conventional foliage of the period. The favourite ornament, the dog-tooth (completely hollowed four-leaf pyramids), may, of course, be found (West Walton, Norfolk, Pl. 18, Skelton, near York, North Riding, and Darrington, West Riding).

Decorated The head of the arch is broader (possibly ogee). Mouldings are not so deeply cut; the arches and sides have many small shallow mouldings, and sometimes there are several small shafts. The capitals might have the natural foliage of the period. The favourite ornament now, the ball-flower (a

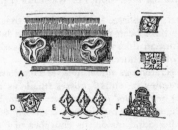

A. 14th-century
ball-flower. B. 14th-century
four-leaved flower.

C. 15th-century square flower. D. Tudor Rose

E. Brattishing. F. Strap-work.

globular flower with three incurved petals) and the four-leaved flower may occur. Heckington, Lincs (Pl. 19), has fine work of this period.

Perpendicular The pointed arch of the doorway under a square hood-mould became most popular (Hilborough, Norfolk) (Pl. 20). The spandrels between the two might have tracery, heraldry or sculpture—angels with censers fit in nicely. The arch often used is the one known as four-centred (struck from four centres, instead of two as previously). If there is ornamentation, it consists of small leaves or flowers of square form, which may occur in the wide shallow hollows now so popular.

Renaissance Doorways of the seventeenth and eighteenth centuries again have round arches, but they are large and they usually have projecting keystones and big arch-stones or voussoirs (Pl. 11).

It must, of course, be remembered that a doorway may have been moved and set in a later wall. (So a Norman doorway does not necessarily make the rest of the church Norman!)

Little scratchings sometimes seen on doorways or elsewhere may be votive crosses (made as evidence of a vow) or masons' or merchants' marks. Scratchings of figures and buildings are known as graffiti, and can be found inside the churches of Compton, Surrey, and Ashwell, Herts (the latter having one of Old St Paul's).

Two large incised figures of a manticore and a leopard on the outside walls of North Cerney, Glos, are unique.

Plate 5 1. Mungrisdale, Cumberland, in a delightful setting
2. Huish Episcopi, Somerset. 3. Leigh-on-Mendip, Somerset
4. Banwell, Somerset. Three of the grand Perpendicular towers of
Somerset, in contrasting styles.

Plate 6 1. St Levan, Cornwall. 2. Poughill, Cornwall. 3 Chelvey, Somerset. 4. Ashburton, Devon, with stair turret in middle of side.

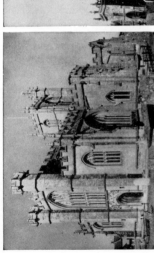

Plate 7
1. Crewkerne, Somerset.
2. Blythburgh, Suffolk, with clerestory prominent.
3. Southwold, Suffolk. Note clerestory and flat parapet of tower. (Three Perpendicular churches.)
4. Marton, Cheshire, a black-and-white 'magpie' church of half-timber and plaster.

Plate 8 1. Seal, Kent, a Perpendicular tower with stair turret projecting above. 2. Runhall, Norfolk, round tower. 3. Filby, Norfolk, showing stepped battlements. 4. Edingthorpe, Norfolk, round tower with octagonal upper storey; thatched roof.

Plate 9 1. Beverley Minster, East Riding, with two Perpendicular west towers. 2. St Mary's, Beverley, showing Perpendicular central tower. 3. Dent, West Riding. 4. Grasmere, Westmorland. Two churches that harmonize with the landscape.

Plate 10 1. Melton Mowbray, Leics, Early English tower with Perpendicular belfry. 2. Earls Barton, Northants, Saxon tower. 3. Haselbech, Northants, having double belfry windows under ogee arch. 4. Lowick, Northants, with octagonal storey on tower.

Plate 11 1. Castor, Northants, Norman tower. 2. West Walton, Norfolk, Early English detached tower. 3. St Vedast, City of London, Wren church with stone spire. 4. Wimborne St Giles, Dorset, a church of the classical style.

Plate 12

1. Brenzett, Kent, timber belfry with spire.
2. Ford, Sussex, timber belfry with cap.
3. East Bergholt, Suffolk, interior of bell cage.
4. Stanford Rivers, Essex, lead spire on timber belfry.

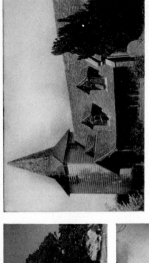

Plate 13

1. Old Romney, Kent, timber spire overlapping tower.
2. Greensted, Essex, tower, spire and Saxon nave of timber.
3. Bapchild, Kent, another overlapping timber spire.
4. Brookland, Kent, detached timber spire.

Plate 14 1. Great Baddow, Essex, lead spire and clerestory of brick. 2. Eynsford, Kent, slender overlapping timber spire. 3. Bampton, Oxon, stone spire with pinnacles and dormer windows. 4. Braunton, Devon, overlapping lead broach spire.

Plate 15 1. Aldwincle St Peter, Northants, broach spire. 2. Weekley, Northants, parapet spire. 3. Hemingborough, East Riding, parapet spire, its height much more than that of the tower. 4. Moulton, Lincs, parapet spire with flying buttresses. The beauty of stone spires.

Plate 16 1. Wilby, Northants, stone spire rising from octagonal storey surmounting tower. 2. Northleach, Glos, a fine porch with turrets, pinnacles and niches. 3. Eltisley, Cambs, parapet spire. 4. Exeter, St Mary Steps, old clock with three jacks.

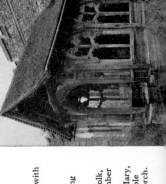

Plate 17

1. Malmesbury Abbey, Wilts. Norman porch (with Apostles).
2. Aston Eyre, Salop. Norman doorway depicting the Entry into Jerusalem.
3. Boxford, Suffolk, 14th-century timber porch.
4. Pulham, St Mary, Norfolk, a notable East Anglian porch.

Plate 18 1. Iffley, Oxon, Norman doorway. 2. West Walton, Norfolk, Early English porch. 3. Heckingham, Norfolk, another Norman doorway. 4. Quenington, Glos, Norman doorway with carved tympanum.

Plate 19 1. Heckington, Lincs, Decorated porch. 2. Baltons-borough, Somerset, door with original door-handle. 3. Dartmouth, Devon, door with 14th-century ironwork; note two leopards. 4. Easthorpe, Essex, Early English lancet windows.

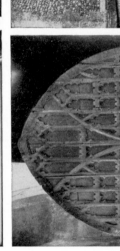

Plate 20

1. Fritton, Suffolk, Norman chancel and 14th-century screen.
2. Ockham, Surrey, Early English lancet windows.
3. Addlethorpe, Lincs, door of Perpendicular period.
4. Hilborough, Norfolk, Perpendicular doorway.

DOORS

These are nearly always massive, with a huge lock and a key several inches long. A door at Hadstock, Essex, is Saxon.

Before the middle of the fourteenth century the smith decorated the door, and his skill was remarkable. Norman ironwork remains on doors at Little Hormead, Herts, Old Woking, Surrey, Edstaston, Salop, and Stillingfleet, East Riding. At Eaton Bray and Turvey, Beds, there are splendid doors of the thirteenth century with iron scrollwork of straps and hinges made by Thomas of Leighton, who made the famous grille for the Queen Eleanor monument in Westminster Abbey. At St Saviour's, Dartmouth, Devon (Pl. 19), the huge door is covered with fourteenth-century ironwork of large leaf scrolls and two leopards.

Later the craft of the wood-worker prevailed (Harpley, Norfolk, and Stoke-by-Nayland, Suffolk) and the ornamentation at the head of the door might follow the window tracery of the period, as at Wellow, Somerset (Reticulated), and Addlethorpe, Lincs (Pl. 20) (Perpendicular).

Very often the original door-handle or knocker remains (Baltonsborough, Somerset) (Pl. 19). At Adel, West Riding, the ring is held in the mouth of a monster swallowing a man, and at Dormington, Herefords, it is held in the mouth of a demon head.

Doors to tower stairways are often original, and even the rood-stairs may have their original door, as at Blewbury, Berks, and Stogumber, Somerset.

If original, windows can be one of the best clues to the date of a church, but it must always be remembered that a window might have been inserted in a much earlier wall. The following are the characteristics of the various periods; the change from one to another was of course gradual, and often one window can combine current and earlier designs. The change was fairly consistent throughout the country.

Saxon   Round-headed, but sometimes triangular-headed. The latter is an infallible clue to this period. The semicircular heads are frequently cut out of a single stone. The sides or jambs may slope slightly towards one another. The earliest Saxon windows were cut straight through the wall with little, if any, splay. Normally a window is flush with the outer wall face and splayed or sloped within, thus enlarging the window opening. There is, however, one exception, for in the later (but not in the latest) Saxon era, windows were sometimes splayed within and without (the glass therefore being set in the middle of the wall) (Tichborne, Hants); this is another infallible clue to date.

Circular openings were sometimes favoured and may be late Saxon or early Norman. The baluster-shaft belfry windows have been mentioned in connection with towers (p. 29).

Norman   The semicircular arch continues and the jambs are now perfectly upright. Proportions vary; generally windows are small owing to the high cost of glass. Larger windows were sometimes treated outside like a doorway, with two orders to the arch and perhaps shafts to the jambs (Barnwell, Cambs).

Windows were usually high up in the walls and equal spacing was not often attempted The east

Saxon. Norman. Early English.
Tichborne, Hants. Barnwell, Cambs. Lancet.

window might be a single small light, as at Elkstone, Glos (Pl. 26), and Fritton, Suffolk (Pl. 20), but occasionally three such lights might be grouped together, as at Darenth, Kent.

Large circular windows may sometimes be found. At Barfreston, Kent, and Castle Hedingham, Essex, a miniature arcade radiates in and from the centre of the window, making a wheel-window. (We might mention here that this was, of course, the forerunner of the rose windows of the Gothic period, which were very popular on the Continent but were rarely favoured in England, two good examples in a village church being at Milton Malsor, Northants;

circular windows, however, continued to be used throughout the medieval period in some East Anglian clerestories, often alternating with ordinary windows, as at Cley, Norfolk.)

Early English The pointed arch is now used for the first time. Tall, narrow windows of the earlier part of this period (around 1220) are called lancets. They are of severe simplicity, but three grouped together at the east end, as often in Sussex (Boxgrove Priory, Burpham and Amberley, Pl. 44; also East-thorpe, Essex, Pl. 19, and Minster, Thanet), make a most pleasing background to the altar. The centre of the three lights usually rises above the others.

Two lancets together at the east end are much less common—Tangmere, Sussex, is an example. Five together, however, can be found (Bosham, Sussex), but special mention must be made of the beautiful chancel ends of Blakeney, Norfolk, and Ockham, Surrey (Pl. 20), where the number is seven.

Tracery, or stone bars, in the heads of the windows was not invented—it gradually evolved itself. A window on its exterior now usually had a hood-mould to protect the window from rain-water. When two lancets each with a hood-mould were grouped together, the dip in the middle would collect water which could only escape over the mould and on to the windows. To avoid this the lancets were enclosed by one hood-mould, and this also enclosed a small piece of wall. When this blank wall was itself pierced (cut in the solid stonework) plate-tracery resulted; the belfry windows of the splendid Early English tower of West Walton, Norfolk (Pl. 11), are good examples. This is therefore the germ of church window tracery.

When such a group forms one window with open-

Plate tracery.
Carlby, Lincs.

Geometrical.
Owmby, Lincs.

ings formed of thin bars of stone above, this is then called bar-tracery, and it became universal. The tracery is supported on vertical bars called mullions.

Plate-tracery, whether with two lancets or three lancets (as at Ripple, Worcs), with the blank space or spaces above pierced with a circle or quatrefoil (four hollows between four cusps), is therefore the origin of the Geometrical window, our first bar-tracery. The church could now for the first time have large windows, which might have seven lights below, giving a large space above for the tracery. The wall was, of course, weakened, but buttresses were given greater projection.

Decorated At the end of the last period and the beginning of this period, the tracery is appropriately called Geometrical, the earliest form being the circle, as at Grantham, Lincs, such circles being uncusped. Later it was usual to add cusps within the circles (Leominster Priory, Herefords, and Corby, Lincs). (A cusp is a projecting point intersecting small arc openings.) Windows with tracery comprising only such circles can usually be dated in the second half of the thirteenth century.

At the end of that century and in the first fifteen years of the fourteenth century other forms exist side by side with the circle or are substituted for it; the long-lobed pointed trefoil is very popular, as are trefoils giving the appearance of daggers (Stoke Golding, Leics). Trefoils might also be round-lobed (Besthorpe, Norfolk). Such tracery might have a centrepiece, but at this time there is also tracery without a centrepiece. It may be: (*a*) Intersecting tracery. From each mullion spring two arched mullions of the same radius as the containing arch and intersecting with one another. The curves may be uncusped (Owmby, Lincs), but more often they are cusped. (*b*) Graduated lancets, usually three or five, rising up to the arch (Middleton Cheney, Northants). Again they may or may not have cusps. They are common in the west of England—Wimborne Minster, Dorset, and Ottery St Mary, Devon.

The ball-flower ornament (common from 1307 to 1327) was used on windows in the Hereford area (Leominster Priory). Each south aisle window of Gloucester Cathedral has as many as 1,400.

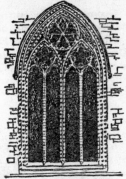

Geometrical.

Corby, Lincs   Leominster Priory,
Herefords

Geometrical.
Stoke Golding, Leics.

Geometrical window tracery is therefore of greater variety than that of any other style.

Slightly later in the Decorated period we have Reticulated or net-like window tracery. The tracery is entirely composed of ogee arches (compound curves, concave and convex—so very popular in the

Left Geometrical, Middleton Cheney, Northants; *centre* Geometrical, Besthorpe, Norfolk; *right* Reticulated, 14th century, Chalgrove, Oxon.

fourteenth century), all producing similar forms, each tier diminishing in number (Beeston-next-Mileham and Norton Subcourse, Pl. 21, Norfolk).

Later still, Flowing tracery became the fashion. Simple geometrical curves (such as circles and trefoils) are still sometimes to be found even amongst the flowing curves, as at Beverley Minster,

but normally they were completely eliminated.
Previously the beauty of tracery lay in the form of
the openings, but now the eye follows the curves
of the bars. There is, of course, infinite variety
in the designs.

South Lincolnshire and the East Riding of Yorkshire have numerous churches of the period of

Left   Ogee arch and Reticulated tracery;
centre Kentish tracery;
right Flowing, Great Horwood, Bucks.

Flowing tracery and therefore abound in good
examples—Sleaford and Heckington, Lincolnshire,
and Patrington, Holy Trinity, Hull and Cottingham,
East Riding. Among village churches we can mention
Ducklington, Oxon, Great Horwood, Bucks, Wymington, Beds, Ringstead, Northants, and Snet-
tisham, Norfolk.

In Kent and occasionally elsewhere a local and beautiful type of tracery is found. It is indeed called Kentish tracery, and consists of an elaborately cusped and indented quatrefoil of starlike form with prominent spikes protruding from it (Chartham, Kent).

Perpendicular In France, Flowing tracery developed into the even more elaborate style known as the Flamboyant, but in England we then had a complete change to straight lines. It began at Gloucester Cathedral and it was indeed a great revolution, for it set the fashion for windows for nearly two hundred years during the great church building period before the Reformation, when the merchant classes were at the height of their prosperity.

Such a window gave the maximum amount of light and every possible scope to the glass-painter, whose art was then reaching its highest point of development. He could insert his figures of saints in the rectangular panels, which was quite impossible with the earlier Flowing tracery.

It is always easy to detect a Perpendicular window. The design is most satisfying, there is infinite variety, and its detailed study is rewarding.

This rectilinear tracery can be seen to perfection in the great East Anglian churches. There are huge east windows, as at Sall, Walpole St Peter (Pl. 42) and St Nicholas, King's Lynn, Norfolk, and Cavendish, Suffolk, and large aisle windows and numerous clerestory windows (p. 15). Necton, Norfolk (Pl. 21), is typical of the area. Rather curiously a small piece of Flowing tracery is often retained in

64

Perpendicular window tracery.

the side lights of the Perpendicular tracery in these parts. That most superb of all buildings, King's College Chapel, Cambridge, is really just a row of Perpendicular windows with buttresses between them to support the fan vault—all completely English.

Perhaps, however, the most beautiful stonework of the windows of the period is to be found in some Somerset churches, such as Curry Rivel and Crowcombe (Pl. 21), and in many east Devon churches such as Cullompton and Kentisbeare. A type peculiar to the extreme West is well seen at St Neot, Cornwall, and Ashburton, Devon.

The vertical bars continuing upward into the head of the window were much stronger than the earlier bars with their geometrical or flowing curves. Advantage was taken of this to increase the size of the window; but mullions now perhaps 50 or 60 feet high had themselves to be stayed to prevent bulge,

15th-century,
Perpendicu-
lar.

15th-century, granite.   15th-century,
West Country   Perpendicular.
Perpendicular.   Dallington, Northants
St Neot, Cornwall.   (with low-side window).

and this was effected by the insertion of horizontal
bars called transoms across the lower lights as well
as in the tracery—again to the great satisfaction of
the glass-painter. A Perpendicular window seems
to be nothing but mullions; a bar from the apex of
an arch is termed a supermullion (above right).

Arches at this time were usually more obtuse, but
the special arch of the period is the four-centred
arch which admirably suited the tracery. Square-
headed windows now occur, and indeed in the
North they are quite common. It must, of course, be
remembered that some fifteenth-century windows
were of the simplest possible type with perhaps no
tracery at all but a few cusps at the tops of the lights.

The delightful Tudor oriel window so often found in houses is rare in churches. The porch of Stoke Dry, Rutland, however, has a charming example.

Post-Reformation The Gothic style lingered in Oxford until the seventeenth century as shown in several college chapels (Wadham), but elsewhere the Renaissance style soon predominated. This produced large plain windows with once again the semicircular arch, often with projecting keystone, as in Wren's City churches. (Wimborne St Giles, Dorset, Pl. 11, shows Post-Reformation windows.)

BUTTRESSES

The earliest buttresses were very wide, but they were

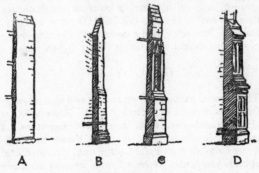

Buttresses.

A. 12th-century, Iffley, Oxon.
B. 13th-century, Higham Ferrers, Northants.
C. 14th-century, Debenham, Suffolk.
D. 15th-century, St Lawrence, Evesham, Worcs.

of such slight projection as to be of little use. The walls, however, were then exceedingly thick. (See p. 17.)

Throughout the medieval period the depth of the buttress increased and the width decreased, corresponding to a decrease in the thickness of the walls. Later ones may be adorned with niches for figures, or panelling. Buttresses were usually sloped off at intervals to shed rainwater.

The corners of a church in the Early English period nearly always had rectangular buttresses, whereas in the Decorated period and later they were usually set diagonally.

If a buttress is poised above an aisle roof and reaches from the clerestory to a buttress on the ground, it is called a flying buttress and indicates that the roof is of stone (vaulted) (Boxgrove Priory, Sussex). Pinnacles might be added to buttresses to give them weight and deflect thrust downwards.

GARGOYLES

These occur particularly on towers and also often on the upper parts of exterior walls. Although not always handsome, they were most necessary. A gargoyle is a projecting spout to throw the rainwater from the gutter clear of the wall. The medieval churchman had a sense of humour and certainly enjoyed his creation of gargoyles, as we can enjoy studying them. They depict fantastic monsters and figures in every possible attitude, and not always with drawing-room manners.

There are really splendid gargoyles at Evercreech

and Monksilver (Pl. 22), Somerset, Winchcombe, Glos, Malpas, Cheshire, Patrington, East Riding, and East Markham, Notts; at the last church one figure has its hand in its wide-open mouth. At Wye, Kent, a snake is held in the mouth, and at Welford, Northants, two figures hold the spout between them. At Denford, in that county, are many gargoyles as well as numerous quaint heads both outside and inside the church.

OTHER EXTERIOR FIGURE SCULPTURE

The Normans were fond of corbel-tables—projecting masonry supported on a row of small corbels,

Corbel-table.
Bossall, North Riding.

Saxon sundial.
Marsh Baldon, Oxon.

usually just underneath the roof. These little corbels were often elaborately carved in the forms of monsters and figures (Kilpeck, Herefords, and Elkstone, Glos). Fascinating corbel-tables can also be well studied at Steeple Langford, Wilts, Bossall, North Riding, and Berkswell, Warwickshire. There is nearly always such a corbel-table at the top of a tower supporting a thirteenth-century stone spire, and for the same reason many of the best later towers had a band of ornament in this position underneath the parapet.

Exterior string-courses of figures or foliage continued to be used from time to time, one of the best examples being at Adderbury, Oxon, with weird animals and birds and figures playing musical instruments. The finest exterior figure sculpture is on the west fronts of Wells and Exeter Cathedrals.

Heads of persons, angels or animals can also often be seen at the ends of hood-moulds—the outer moulding over a window or doorway; these corbel terminations are known as hood-mould stops or label stops.

The cross at the end of a roof gable may be original, and most appropriately it might be a crucifix (Tilty, Essex, Haslingfield, Cambs, and Skelton, near York, North Riding).

The most remarkable external crucifix is the one of Saxon date on a wall at Romsey Abbey, Hants.

MASS DIALS

Scientific sundials on churches generally date from the end of the seventeenth or the beginning of the eighteenth century. Rather curiously about twenty Saxon ones remain, the most famous being at Kirkdale, North Riding.

Mass dials or scratch dials were constructed differently and they vary in form, size, detail and position in the most remarkable manner. They all, however, have a central hole, in which the gnomon or style was fixed and from which the lines, if any, radiate. One line is often better marked than the others, namely 9 a.m.—the usual hour for Mass. It is no use, of course, looking on the north wall for them as the sun rarely reaches that part. Occasionally figures for the hours are incised, as at Farmington, Glos. Mass dials are most common around the Cotswolds and in Somerset and Hampshire.

A number of small square holes, particularly on a tower, seem to have no purpose. They are, however, putlog holes, in which the scaffolding was erected, and they have never been filled in to this day (Great Burstead, Essex, and East Hendred, Berks).

DEDICATION

Without going near a church, one can obtain much joy in making lists of dedications under counties. Every church is, of course, dedicated to Almighty God, and to Him alone. To give a church a name, however, was useful, and in a town it was helpful in distinguishing it from other churches. The dedication was in memory of a saint or an event. The first seven in order of popularity for old churches are St Mary, All Saints, St Peter, St Michael, St Andrew, St John the Baptist, and St Nicholas. The last therefore beats St Paul and the Holy Trinity (both much favoured in the nineteenth century).

So often a saint that had a dramatic death (St Lawrence on a gridiron, for example) was far more popular than a person who simply wrote, even if it was the Gospels; and so three of the Evangelists are low, St John alone retrieving his position through also being an Apostle, and one who was much loved.

Even if a saint is popular, it by no means indicates that he is equally popular over the whole country. The majority have groups of churches in one particular area. Out of nearly 400 old churches in Kent, for example, only four are dedicated to St Andrew (Buckland, Sibertswold, Tilmanstone and Wickhambreux, and all are in the extreme east of the county). This is even more remarkable considering that the cathedral at Rochester is dedicated to him. To arrive at fifth place in the national order therefore means that considerable leeway must be made up somewhere—and it certainly is in south Lincolnshire and East Anglia.

Most Cornish churches are dedicated to a saint with a delightful name, but of whom one has never heard. He or she was no doubt the Celtic missionary who founded that particular church.

PLAN
(See pages 2 and 3)

The plan of a church is really its most consistent part, for it was not dependent upon geology, and the requirements of worshippers in Northumberland were the same as those in Cornwall and Kent.

The High Altar was and is the focal point. Space for at least two more altars had to be found and also a route for processions. The Christian Church has always tried to be practical and to carry out Our Lord's Command at the Last Supper. "Do this", which does not necessarily mean everyone sitting still. The need for several altars may be partly due

72

to a general observance of the rule which is still observed in the Greek Church, that an altar should not be used for the Eucharist more than once a day, and, of course, a priest (and there might be several) had to say a Mass each day.

Increase in population and wealth were really the only reasons for making enlargements. Many of the Norman and Early English churches of Sussex have never had to be enlarged.

Stewkley, Bucks, has not had to be altered since it was built in Norman times. On the other hand in East Anglia, owing to the wealth of the wool trade, earlier churches were sometimes swept away in the Perpendicular period, and glorious churches in that style erected in their place. These do not usually show any earlier structure, but otherwise the church often shows gradual changes, although its form may be dictated by the original church.

The simplest plan is nave and chancel only. The word nave, indicating where the congregation sit, is derived from the Latin word for a ship (*navis*)—the Church being a refuge on life's troubled waters. Some Norman churches had another compartment between nave and chancel called the choir (nothing to do with those who sing). Above this might be a tower, as at Stewkley, Bucks, and Studland, Dorset.

Transepts (chapels at right angles to the main building) might have been added by the Normans to their central tower—thus producing the cruciform plan. This plan gradually became less popular, but it was always liked in the Wilts, Berkshire Downs, and north Chilterns areas (Ivinghoe, Bucks).

73

Two extremely pleasing Perpendicular examples are at Minster Lovell, Oxon, and Poynings, Sussex. The great churches of the East Riding usually have a central tower (St Mary's, Beverley) (Pl. 9). When the tower is central, a large west window is then possible, and this, of course, gives additional light inside the church (Crewkerne, Somerset) (Pl. 7).

The earliest churches on the Continent had a round east end called an apse, which was derived from the Roman basilica. The Celtic Church had always used a square east end and this type almost completely prevailed after the early Norman period. Many apses no doubt were altered to square ends, and many central towers must have been taken down and a new tower erected in the more favoured position at the west end. An apse still remains at Hales, Norfolk (Pl. 21), and Fritton, Suffolk (Pl. 20).

If additional accommodation was required the church was enlarged in any way possible. One of the side walls of the nave could be set back, but more often an aisle was built. The Norman church could, of course, have been built with aisles, as at St Margaret-at-Cliffe, Kent, and St Peter's, Northampton. The aisle wall may have been built first and then the arches made, being cut through the nave wall without taking it down. This upper wall (not having been altered) may therefore be the oldest part of the church and there may even be traces of the earlier windows. (Another good place at which to look for evidence of an earlier church is outside at the junction of nave and chancel.)

If another aisle was then necessary, it would be added in the same way on the other side (both aisles possibly absorbing transepts; transepts remaining are common in the West Country). It may be wider than the earlier one, but that also might later be widened. With wider aisles, the side windows were further from the centre and additional height was necessary for the roof, and clerestories were therefore heightened (the old windows being now within the church) or added for the first time.

With the increase of wealth of the merchant classes in the fifteenth and early sixteenth centuries, chantry chapels and guild chapels became popular, and aisles might therefore now be added to the chancel for these purposes, so that the final plan is a large parallelogram divided lengthwise by two arcades (the only projections being tower and porch).

Some churches are called round churches. Actually only the nave is round. They were built under the influence of the Knights Templars and Hospitallers in imitation of the church of the Holy Sepulchre at Jerusalem. There are four: Temple Church, City of London, and at Cambridge, Northampton and Little Maplestead, Essex.

Provision for altars and processions was the main factor governing the plan of medieval churches and cathedrals. A procession is a great act of worship and, of course, affected the planning of medieval churches—more particularly the greater churches, in providing the necessary processional path or aisles around the whole. In every church there was a Sunday procession around the church inside and often outside, leaving by the north door and entering again by the south door. One of these doorways (probably the one on the north) is now often blocked up. The principal entrance to a parish church (unlike a cathedral) was not by the west door—many churches do not even have such a door, let alone protect it by a porch. (Eynsford, Kent, Pl. 14, and Yapton, Sussex, have examples of west porches, and Higham Ferrers, Northants, has a notable west entrance.)

The special occasions for great processions are Palm Sunday, Corpus Christi, Rogation days (and around the fields as well) and Candlemas (2nd February). There can have been few more joyful occasions or more beautiful sights than such a procession. The thurifer with incense was followed by the richly jewelled processional cross surrounded by burning tapers, and then the priests wearing marvellous copes preceding a number of brightly embroidered banners of best English work; finally there would have been the Sacred Host or a relic under a gorgeous canopy. The people joined in, and sang joyfully, for worship was joyous.

ROOFS (INTERIOR)

Roofs are of wood. Roofs of stone are called vaults and are referred to later. The most simple form is the high-pitched single framed trussed rafter roof in which each pair of rafters is a complete truss in itself (South Burlingham, Norfolk). The king-post roof is of this type, but with a strong beam from wall to wall on the centre of which stands the king-post. This post supports a central purlin which helps to support the collars. Many king-post roofs remain in the small ancient churches of the

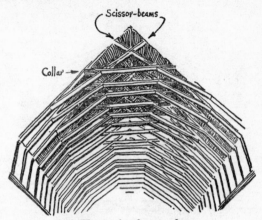

Trussed rafter roof.
South Burlingham, Norfolk.

south-east and may date back to the thirteenth or fourteenth century (Lyminster, Sussex, and Barking, Suffolk).

Later roofs were usually double framed with principal tie-beams placed at intervals. In a fairly flat tie-beam roof the pitch of the roof can be obtained in three ways: (*a*) the tie-beam is itself completely cambered or pitched (Crewkerne, Somerset); (*b*) the upper part only of the tie-beam is pitched, known as firred-beam (Blythburgh, Suffolk, Pl. 22); both these types are seen at Denston, Suffolk (Pl. 44); or (*c*) the centre of the beam is surmounted by a small post which "pushes" the centre of the roof upwards (Leigh-on-Mendip, Somerset)

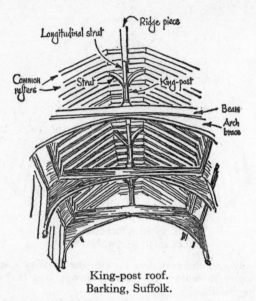

King-post roof.
Barking, Suffolk.

(Pl. 22). Somerset has many wonderful examples of tie-beam roofs, as at Martock, Evercreech, Wellow, Weston Zoyland, Somerton (Pl. 22), Leigh-on-Mendip (Pl. 22), High Ham, Long Sutton and St Cuthbert's, Wells.

A steeply pitched tie-beam roof may have king-posts (Adderbury, Oxon), or instead of a single king-post a pair of struts or posts called queen-posts (Addlethorpe, Lincs), or no posts at all (Ufford, Suffolk).

Sometimes the tie-beam is itself supported on

arched braces which may have traceried spandrels.

The tie-beam roof is constructionally the best type of church roof.

Sometimes a roof may be boarded or ceiled between the principal rafters and have bosses (often brightly coloured and gilt) at the intersections of the rafters (Astbury and Northwich, Cheshire). Each panel may occasionally be carved with a design (Somerton, Pl 22, Somerset). The most remarkable example of this treatment is at Shepton Mallet, Somerset: there are 350 panels with a design only duplicated once. This roof is rounded, called a wagon roof, which is the universal type in the West Country. Sometimes all the rafters of a wagon roof are now exposed, but this is not correct, for the space between the principals should be plastered, giving a homely effect (Selworthy, Somerset) (Pl. 23). When carved panels of a roof are coloured and gilt, the result is magnificent, as can be seen at Cullompton, Devon.

Coloured bosses on a plastered wagon roof are most effective, as at Meavy, Devon. Bosses of wood, as of stone on a vault, are often carved with a variety of figures and subjects and are of great interest (Sampford Courtenay, Devon). A series at Sall, Norfolk, depict scenes from the life of Our Lord.

The most ornamental type of roof is, however, the hammer-beam variety which is almost confined to the eastern counties. A hammer-beam is the projecting beam from which the main arch of the roof springs, and the span is ingeniously reduced in width accordingly with a minimum of outward thrust. In a double hammer-beam roof there are two tiers of such beams on each side. There are usually an immense number of angels, often over a hundred, and one almost feels as if they are flying above. Wonderful examples can be seen at Knapton, Swaffham, Cawston, Tilney All Saints and Gissing, Norfolk, Woolpit (Pl. 24), Badingham (Pl. 24), Earl Stonham (Pl. 23), Grundisburgh, Hopton (near Diss) and Worlingworth, Suffolk, March, Cambs, and Great Bromley, Essex.

Arch-braced roof with collar.
Yaxley, Suffolk.

Sometimes, unfortunately, the angels have disappeared or are damaged. They were favourite targets for Cromwell's soldiers, as has been proved at the glorious church of South Creake, Norfolk, where bullets have been found inside them!

The double-framed arch-braced roof is common anywhere (except in the West Country). There is almost invariably a collar-beam across the top which prevents thrust (spreading outwards), but very curiously in Norfolk, where this type of roof was most popular, a local feature is to omit this collar-beam (North Elmham). This no doubt explains why

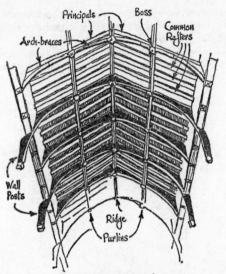

Arch-braced roof.
North Elmham, Norfolk.

many roofs in that county have had to be renewed.

A roof can, of course, combine several different types, as at Mildenhall, Suffolk (tie-beam and hammer-beam).

Bere Regis, Dorset, has a remarkable roof with huge bosses, and large painted figures of the Twelve Apostles (St Peter being illustrated on Pl. 24). The most astonishing medieval wooden roof is, however, at Needham Market, Suffolk.

The base of the roof above the wall on either

side formed a cornice (wall-plate). In East Anglia this was often carved with angels (Earl Stonham, Suffolk, Pl. 23) and in the West with foliage.

Aisle roofs were usually of simple design, being lean-to from wall to wall. They could be adorned

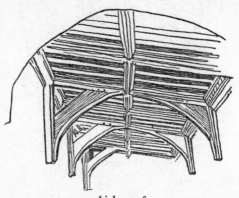

Aisle roof.
South Acre, Norfolk.

with angels and figures, and sometimes there was a large spandrel filled with lace-like tracery.

The wall-posts of a roof (for preventing thrust), whether of the main roof or that of an aisle, nearly always rest on corbels, which are usually of stone and should be carefully studied, for they are full of interest and often amusing. They are often human heads, angels or grotesque monsters (Sharrington, Norfolk) (Pl. 23). They should be coloured as at Great Henny, Essex, Bradford Abbas, Dorset, and the four fine musicians at Duston, Northants. Occasionally a face may have glass eyes which wink as one walks along (Cley, Norfolk, and Maids Moreton, Bucks).

The eastern end of the nave roof may be more elaborately carved or coloured than the remainder of the roof. This would be a rood celure, and will be noted later (p. 128).

Even angels on roofs differ in different localities. Broadly speaking, in East Anglia they have very outspread wings, and in the West Country the wings are far more vertical or closed up.

At this point we must mention colour. To appreciate the original beauty of church roofs we must remember that, as with most other parts of the church, they were ablaze with the most gorgeous colours and gilt. From remains of such colour we know that the work in this respect was perfect. It was done for the glory of God and was therefore inspired.

When colour in church is mentioned one tends to think of bad Victorian glass and the often hopeless wall-paintings and mosaics of that period. It is difficult to realize that the colouring everywhere was once so beautiful.

VAULTS

Arched roofs of stone are called vaults and these are usually confined to cathedrals and greater churches. A small part of a church such as a porch or a tower, particularly a tower in Somerset, may, however, be vaulted in even the most simple church.

Whilst the arch was round, as in Saxon and Norman times, the vault followed suit and this greatly restricted its scope. With the introduction of the pointed arch, however, vaulting was revolutionized, as any span could then be covered.

The simplest vault known to the Normans was the round barrel vault, or a tunnel. By two barrel vaults intersecting, a groined vault is obtained, as at Darenth, Kent.

A vault is constructed on a temporary wooden structure called centering; when the ribs were made as real arches centering was only necessary for the intervening spaces (called cells).

The simplest arrangement is quadripartite, two tranverse ribs enclosing two diagonal ones crossing one another and thereby forming four cells. This was common in Norman and Early English times (Boxgrove Priory, Sussex, and Christchurch Priory, Hants, Pl. 24). When additional ribs were introduced (such as ridge ribs and tiercerons), the cells increased in number and decreased in size. Ridge ribs follow the ridges, and tierceron ribs spring from the same point as the transverse and diagonal arches, but rise not to the central boss but to some point on one of the ridge ribs (Exeter Cathedral).

In the fourteenth century, ribs were introduced for the first time which did not have some constructional object; they were mainly decorative and they did not spring from the wall, as previously, but crossed the spandrels from rib to rib thereby making elaborate star-like patterns. Such a vault is known as a lierne vault; Tewkesbury Abbey (Pl. 25) and Norwich Cathedral have wonderful examples.

In the fifteenth century a most beautiful form of vault was introduced. It is the fan vault, and it is purely English. In such a vault all the ribs are of identical curve and are spaced at equal angles with one another. The ribs have lost their former

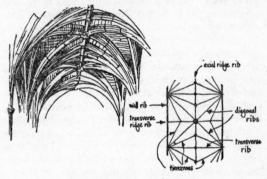

Tierceron vault.

structural use, for they are now carved out of the slab instead of supporting it. The spaces between the cones or fans make diamond-shaped panels. The finest fan vault is in the superb chapel of King's College, Cambridge. Henry VII's Chapel, Westminster Abbey, is a close rival. Sherborne Abbey, Dorset (Pl. 25), is also notable, but equally lovely, though smaller, fan vaults exist at Cullompton, Devon, and North Leigh, Oxon.

An enlarged keystone at the intersection of the ribs of a vault or wooden roof is called a boss. It weighted the ribs and prevented them from rising.

In some later vaults some bosses are effectively prolonged downwards and are called pendants (Divinity School, Oxford, and Ottery St Mary, Devon).

In the whole of English Gothic architecture, it is doubtful if there is any more amazing work than the sculpture on vault bosses. There may be several hundred in one cathedral (Norwich) or church. The majority are so high that details cannot be seen from the ground, yet all the details are there, and this again surely proves that all this was done for God and not for man—hence its beauty. To give one example: on a boss at Tewkesbury of the Birth of Christ, the figure of St Mary is shown wearing a bracelet on each wrist. The illustration from Sherborne Abbey, Dorset (Pl. 26), is of a boss of a mermaid with her comb and looking-glass. Biblical and other subjects are portrayed, and the chief events in Our Lord's life may be depicted on a series of half a dozen or so bosses. Foliage and grotesques are also common, and a sow and litter are favourites.

Photography and binoculars are now able to reveal this beauty to us for the first time.

PIERS AND ARCHES
(Medieval Styles)

(Reference should also be made to the section on Doorways)

If there were no aisles, then there would be no arcades. An arch between nave and chancel called the chancel arch is, however, almost universal, except in Cornwall and parts of Devon, where the churches are in one unbroken line, originally divided by a

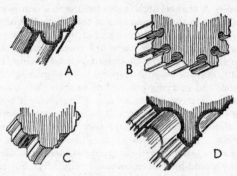

Mouldings.

A. 12th century.   B. 13th century.
C. 14th century.   D. 15th century.
(See also page 161.)

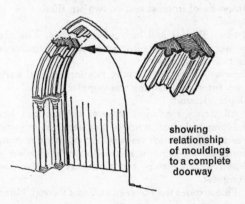

showing
relationship
of mouldings
to a complete
doorway

screen. A chancel arch is also lacking in a number of churches in the Craven area of the North Riding.

An arch is usually supported on a pier, which itself consists of four parts: the abacus from which the arch springs, the capital immediately below, the shaft, and the base. A respond is a half pier against a wall and carrying one end of an arch. All periods had distinctive ornament and foliage, and if these are present then dating will be easy. The majority of churches, however, have very simple pillars and arches which only differ in different periods in the arrangement of their grooves called mouldings (they would have been coloured originally), but two orders just chamfered are common in Gothic. The study of mouldings is therefore most important.

Between each arch and forming a stop to the hood-mould of the arch is often a stone figure. It may be a human head, angel or animal, but it will always be of interest and no two are alike.

Saxon
Arches Round and only of one order. The arch springs from massive impost blocks (the equivalent later of the abacus).
Capitals May have crude, but interesting, sculpture. Interlaced carving was popular.
Shafts Round.

All stones are large. Exterior corners may have the long-and-short work of the later Saxon period (see p. 29). Exterior walls of herring-bone masonry (forming zig-zags) are usually an indication of Saxon workmanship, but they may be just post-Conquest.

Fine arcades may be seen at Great Paxton, Hunts.

Saxon.
Hovingham,
North Riding.

Norman.
Bicker, Lincs.

A notable chancel arch is at Wittering, Northants.

Complete churches: St Lawrence's, Bradford-on-Avon, Wilts, Worth, Sussex (Pl. 26), Brixworth, Northants (probably the oldest complete church still used), Wing, Bucks, Deerhurst, Glos, Escomb, Jarrow and Monkwearmouth, County Durham, Kirk Hammerton, West Riding, Boarhunt, Breamore and Corhampton, Hants, and Bradwell-on-Sea and Greensted (nave of timber) (Pl. 13), Essex.

Saxon crosses have been noted on p. 9. Wirksworth, Derbyshire, has a marvellous Saxon coffinlid, and Breedon-on-the-Hill, Leics, has an amazing Saxon frieze. A remarkable Saxon panel of the crucifixion remains at Daglingworth, Glos (Pl. 27).

Norman

Arches Round and usually of several recessed orders. Often plain with square edges earlier, but

89

Norman
cushion capital.

Volute capitals.
Late Norman.
Harmston, Lincs.

later semicircular rolls, or ornamented as are the
arches of doorways (p. 50).

Abacus Square, or occasionally follows the plan
of the pier. It is always square-edged on top.

Capitals Of three types;
   (*a*) cushion—square above and round below;
   (*b*) scalloped—as last, but cut with vertical flutes;
   (*c*) volute—four leaves springing from the neck,
       bending over under the angles of the square
       part and ending in volutes; late Norman.

Sometimes capitals had elaborate sculpture, as at
Stoke Dry, Rutland, St Peter's, Northampton, and
Wakerley, Northants, and Liverton, North Riding
(Pl. 26).

Shafts Usually massive and cylindrical, but sometimes square with recesses or small circular shafts
at corners, or larger semicircular half-shafts on the
faces. Later shafts may be octagonal.

Bases Insignificant; usually square and sometimes the projecting corners were covered with a leaf ornament.

Fine arcades may be seen at St Peter's, Northampton, and St Margaret-at-Cliffe, Kent. There is a magnificent chancel arch at Tickencote, Rutland, but numerous ones remain, as at Kirkburn and North Grimston, East Riding, Brayton, West Riding, Stoneleigh, Warwicks, Amberley, Sussex (Pl. 44) and Elkstone, Glos (Pl. 26).

Complete churches: Kilpeck and Moccas, Herefords, Heath Chapel, Salop, Barfreston, Kent, Iffley, Oxon (Pl. 18), Stewkley, Bucks, Old Shoreham, Sussex, St Margaret-at-Cliffe, Kent, Studland, Dorset, Avington, Berks, Melbourne and Steetley, Derbyshire, and Adel and Birkin, West Riding.

Norman scalloped capital.   Transitional.
Islip, Oxon.   Buildwas Abbey, Salop

Much Wenlock Priory, Salop.

Transitional Norman

Small ornamental arcades of intersecting round arches produce pointed arches (Much Wenlock Priory, Salop). The pointed arch was invariably used in Gothic architecture. Transitional churches show the gradual change from one style to the other and often a mixture of both. Such churches abound in Sussex, as at Boxgrove Priory, Burpham and New Shoreham.

Early English
Arches Pointed; usually acute arch.
Mouldings Deeply undercut rounds and hollows.
Abacus Almost always round with rounded upper edge and deeply undercut.
Capitals Either moulded or with exquisite conventional stiff-leaf foliage usually with long stalks (Studham and Eaton Bray, Pl. 25, Beds, and East Hendred, Berks). Occasionally human heads are carved amidst the foliage.
Shafts Generally round, often alternating with octagonal; sometimes four semicircles, or four or more slender Purbeck marble shafts, often detached, are placed around a circular pier.

Capitals.

<table>
<tr><td>13th century.
Ingoldmells, Lincs.</td><td>14th century.
Gt Missenden, Bucks.</td></tr>
</table>

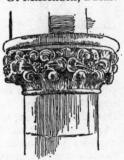

13th-century Foliage Capitals.

Studham, Beds.   East Hendred, Berks.

Bases Deeply cut moulding known as the water-holding moulding.

Ornament Dog-tooth (a completely hollowed four-leaf pyramid, page 52). Trefoil arch, p. 159.

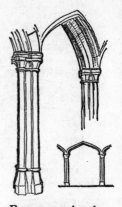

Four-centred arch.
15th century.
St Teath, Cornwall.
Typical West Country.

13th century.
Eaton Bray, Beds.

Fine arcades with foliage may be seen at Eaton
Bray, Beds (Pl. 25), Ivinghoe, Bucks, Slimbridge,
Glos, and Sedgefield, County Durham.

Complete churches: West Walton, Norfolk (Pls.
11 and 18), Uffington, Berks, Clymping, Sussex,
Warmington, Northants, Skelton, near York, North
Riding, and Bottesford, Lincs.

Decorated
Arches Pointed, but not usually so acutely as in
the last style.
Mouldings More numerous, but not so deeply cut
and few hollows. The scroll moulding is usual; the

14th-century capital.   15th-century capital
Westhall, Suffolk.

14th-century base.
Exeter Cathedral.

upper portion is rounded off, and overlaps the lower portion which has an ogee curve.

Abacus It is now really absorbed in the capital by the abolition of the undercut hollow; the upper edge is still rounded.

Capitals Moulded capitals are now usually composed of three members: (i) a top group of two rolls

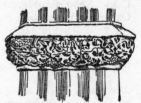

Foliage capitals.

14th-century.   15th-century.
Patrington, East Riding.   Molland, Devon.

of scroll mouldings, the lower being of the same or slightly less projection; (ii) bell; (iii) necking. They are octagonal or circular according to the shaft and may be wholly moulded or have life-like foliage of oak, ivy, maple and vine leaves.

Shafts Usually octagonal, but sometimes circular or four semicircular half-shafts attached to a central square pier, or there are eight half-shafts.

Bases A pair or triplet of rolls.

Ornament Ballflower (a globular flower with three incurved petals) and four-leaved flower (p. 53). The ogee arch (concave and convex curves), p. 63, and crockets are popular. Diaper (foliage wall pattern).
    Fine arcades with foliage capitals may be seen at Patrington, East Riding, Stoke Golding, Leics, and Oakham, Rutland. The foliage of the period can also be seen to perfection at Southwell Minster, Notts.
    Complete churches: Patrington, East Riding, Heckington (Pl. 19), Holbeach, Ewerby and Swaton, Lincs, Shottesbrooke, Berks, Dorchester Abbey, Oxon, and Winchelsea, Sussex.

Perpendicular
Arches Pointed, but still more obtuse, and the four-centred arch is now common.

Mouldings Wide and shallow. The principal mouldings are the casement and double ogee.

Capitals The upper roll of the top group instead of a rounded edge now has an overlapping slanting

15th-century base.
Bloxham, Oxon.

chamfer; other mouldings then decrease downwards in projection; sometimes a necking. Capitals are usually octagonal or many sided even if the shaft is circular. Foliage is mostly confined to the West Country; elsewhere capitals are usually moulded. Undulating foliage surrounding the capital is popular in Devon (Wolborough, Broad Clyst and Molland, Pl. 32) and in Cornwall small leaves often occur on each face of the capital (St Veep).

Shafts Simple octagonal shafts are now usual, but there are two common and distinctive local types:

(*a*) West Country. Four semicircular half-shafts connected by wave mouldings (St Teath, Cornwall).

(*b*) East Anglia. Semicircular half-shafts alternating with wide shallow hollows (casement mouldings), the former alone having small capitals and bases, the hollows continuing up into corresponding hollows in the arch. As the arch is now blunt, the pier occupies a large proportion of the total height of an arcade (Denston, Suffolk) (Pl. 44).

Bases Often polygonal and the outline of a bracket (or double ogee form of moulding) on an unmoulded octagon on a high plinth.

Ornament Four-leaved flower continues but often square and in the hollows now popular; brattishing (a cresting of upright leaves); Tudor Rose.

Fine arcades may be seen at Sall, Swanton Morley, Upton and Shelton, Norfolk, Denston, Suffolk (Pl. 44), Cirencester, Glos (Pl. 25), and Wolborough and Broad Clyst, Devon.

Complete churches: Sall, Walpole St Peter (Pl. 42), Terrington St Clement, and St Nicholas's, King's Lynn, Norfolk, Blythburgh (Pl. 7), Southwold (Pl. 7), Long Melford, Stoke-by-Nayland and Woodbridge, Suffolk, Thaxted, Essex, Crewkerne, Somerset (Pl. 7), St Mary Redcliffe, Bristol, Cirencester (Pl. 25), Chipping Campden, Fairford, Northleach (Pl. 16) and Thornbury, Glos, Ewelme, Oxon, Louth and Tattershall, Lincs, Maids Moreton and Hillesden, Bucks, Cullompton and Tiverton, Devon (both with outside carvings of ships and symbols of the wool trade), Tickhill, West Riding, Thirsk, North Riding, and Alnwick, Northumberland. The beautiful church of Edington, Wilts, is an early example.

Medieval arcades were nearly always of stone, but a fourteenth-century example of timber remains at Selmeston, Sussex, and in Tudor and later times that material was very occasionally used. Wooden arcades also exist at Lower Peover, Cheshire, Wingham, Kent, Langley Marish, Bucks, and Shenfield and Theydon Garnon, Essex.

Renaissance After the Reformation, the Gothic style was gradually superseded by the very different style of the Renaissance based upon Classical traditions. The arch is again round, and the piers follow one of the Classical Orders (the capitals giving clues as to the Orders: Doric and Tuscan, plain and simple, Ionic, with volutes, Corinthian, with rows of acanthus leaves, and Composite, with the features of the Ionic and Corinthian capitals combined). Cherubs and garlands abound.

Complete churches of the one style (often with their contemporary fittings intact) can be seen as follows:

Late seventeenth century: Wren's churches in the City of London (and his charming chapel at Pembroke College, Cambridge), Ingestre, Staffs, and Willen, Bucks.

Eighteenth century: Avington, Hants, Gayhurst, Bucks (adjoining the fine Elizabethan house), Great Witley, Worcs, Blandford and Wimborne St Giles (Pl. 11), Dorset, and several in Shrewsbury, as at St Chad's.

For medieval churches containing seventeenth- and eighteenth-century fittings, see p. 121.

We usually associate the country church with the

medieval style, but one can sometimes find some charming small churches in the Renaissance style in remote country, such as Mungrisdale (Pl. 5) in the Fells of Cumberland: it is lime-washed a bright white outside, and the inside is delightfully light with clear glass which also enables one to see the beauty of the mountains. Similarly Brougham, Westmorland, is of 1660 with all its fittings of that date.

Little Gidding, isolated in fields in Huntingdonshire, was built in the time of Charles I by Nicholas Ferrar in connection with his revival of semi-monastic life. The seats are arranged facing one another, as in a college chapel, an arrangement found again in the remarkable interior of slightly later date at Teigh, Rutland.

Rather different from churches of one date and style are those, far more numerous, which show several or many styles. It is then exciting to attempt to discover the chronological sequence. For churches showing all the medieval periods, visits are recommended to Leominster Priory, Herefords, St Michael's, St Albans, Herts, Bishop's Cleeve, Glos, Burford, Oxon, Stoke-sub-Hamdon, Somerset, and Tansor, Northants. It is easy to distinguish the different periods at Drax and Campsall, West Riding.

INTERIOR ELEVATION

A clerestory normally exists only if there is an aisle below it. It gives additional light to the nave when aisle windows are not sufficient for the purpose. As mentioned, they are most popular in East Anglia, but unpopular in the extreme West, and not common in the extreme South. Clerestories were often added or heightened in the fifteenth century to give additional light to the great rood or crucifix above the rood-screen.

In the greater churches in Norman times there was a third interior storey called the triforium or blind-storey (Christchurch Priory, Hants) (Pl. 24). Situated between arcade and clerestory, it merely looked into the dark space under the aisle roof, and therefore did not admit any light; it was usually abandoned in the later medieval period.

FONTS

We are admitted into the Church by baptism. The font is therefore nearly always at the west end. Several of Saxon date remain (Little Billing, Northants, Deerhurst, Glos, and Curdworth, Warwicks). Saxon crosses made into fonts exist at Dolton, Devon, and Melbury Bubb, Dorset. If the illustration of the latter (Pl. 27) is turned upside-down, then the figures make sense.

There are fortunately innumerable Norman fonts, since even if a church has been rebuilt it may never have been necessary to alter this feature. The font may therefore be medieval in churches that have lost all traces of their medieval foundation, and this point should always be borne in mind.

Norman fonts are massive as immersion was then the practice. They are often amazingly fine and are usually elaborately carved with the ornament of the time (see Doorways p. 50) and with weird and wonderful monsters and figures, and sometimes Old and New Testament scenes.

The East Riding has, in two remote Wold villages, magnificent examples, Cowlam (the Wise Men are splendid) and Langtoft (the martyrdom of St Lawrence on his gridiron is most vivid), and also Kirkburn and North Grimston (the Last Supper is realistic). There is another outstanding group in north-west Norfolk (Shernborne, Toftrees, South Wootton and Sculthorpe), and quite a distinctive group of chalice-shaped fonts at and around Aylesbury, Bucks (Great Kimble).

There are also two groups of late Norman fonts in Cornwall which deserve mention:

(*a*) a cup-bowl elaborately carved and supported on a massive central stem; four angle shafts rise outside the bowl and support heads projecting from the corners (Bodmin, Roche, Pl. 28, and St Austell).

(*b*) a font following the form of a Norman capital and having roundels on the bowl and large heads at the corners (Altarnun, Pl. 44, St Thomas-by-Launceston and Laneast).

Two Norman fonts in Herefordshire must particularly be mentioned—Castle Frome (Pl. 28, showing it squashing evil figures) and Eardisley (Pl. 27). At Stanton Fitzwarren, Wilts, and Southrop, Glos, are fine Norman fonts, with figures of virtues trampling on vices, the names of the vices being inscribed backwards. Other notable fonts of this period are at Lenton, Notts, Bridekirk, Cumber-

Plate 21 1. Necton, Norfolk. 2. Crowcombe, Somerset. Two Perpendicular windows. 3. Hales, Norfolk, round tower, thatched roofs and apse. 4. Norton Subcourse, Norfolk, Decorated window with Reticulated tracery.

Plate 22   1. Blythburgh, Suffolk.   2. Leigh-on-Mendip, Somerset.
3. Monksilver, Somerset, gargoyles.   4. Somerton, Somerset. Three
beautiful tie-beam roofs.

Plate 23

1. Sharrington, Norfolk, corbel.
2. Earl Stonham, Suffolk, cornice carved with angels.
3. Stowlangtoft, Suffolk, rood celure.
4. Selworthy, Someret, plastered wagon roof.

Plate 24 1. Christchurch Priory, Hants, vaulted roof, showing quadripartite arrangement of ribs. 2. Badingham, Suffolk. Hammer-beam roof. 3. Bere Regis, Dorset, part of roof, with painted figure of St Peter. 4. Woolpit, Suffolk. Hammer-beam roof.

Plate 25 1. Sherborne Abbey, Dorset, fan vault. 2. Eaton Bray, Beds, Early English capitals with stiff-leaf foliage. 3. Tewkesbury Abbey, Glos, lierne vault. 4. Cirencester, Glos, Perpendicular piers and arches.

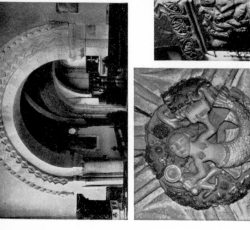

Plate 26

1. Elkstone, Glos, Norman chancel arch.
2. Worth, Sussex, Saxon piers and arches.
3. Sherborne Abbey, Dorset, vault boss of a mermaid with a comb and looking-glass.
4. Liverton, North Riding, Norman capitals with elaborate sculpture.

Plate 27 1. Eardisley, Herefords, Norman font. 2. Daglingworth, Glos, Saxon panel of Crucifixion. 3. Walsoken, Norfolk, Seven Sacrament font. 4. Melbury Bubb, Dorset, font made from Saxon cross; the figures are now upside-down.

Plate 28

Three Norman fonts:
1. Roche, Cornwall.
2. Castle Frome, Herefords, bowl squashing evil monsters (note Baptism of Christ).
3. Ashover, Derbyshire, lead.
4. Sloley, Norfolk, panel of Confirmation on 15th-century font.

Plate 29 1. Surlingham, Norfolk, 15-century font; typically East Anglian. 2. Banwell, Somerset, Norman font (15th-century carving) with Jacobean cover. 3. Trunch, Norfolk, medieval font canopy. 4. Well, North Riding, font cover.

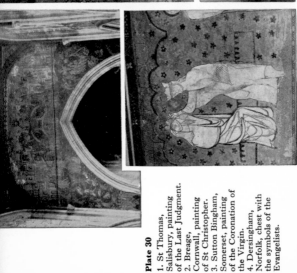

Plate 30

1. St Thomas, Salisbury, painting of the Last Judgment.
2. Breage, Cornwall, painting of St Christopher.
3. Sutton Bingham, Somerset, painting of the Coronation of the Virgin.
4. Dersingham, Norfolk, chest with the symbols of the Evangelists.

Plate 31   1. Wiggenhall St Mary the Virgin, Norfolk, poppy-head bench-ends.   2. Braunton, Devon, square-headed bench-end with Instruments of the Passion.   3. Brent Knoll, Somerset, bench-end showing Reynard the Fox.   4. Great Walsingham, Norfolk, poppy-head bench-ends.

Plate 32 1. Molland, Devon, box-pews. 2. Isleham, Cambs, brass eagle lectern. 3. Detling, Kent, wooden lectern. 4. Astbury Cheshire, wooden eagle lectern.

Plate 33 1. Bishop's Lydeard, Somerset, Jacobean wooden pulpit.
2. Banwell, Somerset, medieval stone pulpit. 3. Stoke St Gregory,
Somerset, Carolean pulpit showing Father Time. 4. Burnham
Norton, Norfolk, wooden pulpit, 1475.

Plate 34 1. Ashton, Devon, panels at base of rood-screen. 2 Lapford, Devon. 3. Bramfield, Suffolk. Two 15th-century wooden rood-screens. 4. Tawstock, Devon, hour-glass.

Plate 35

1. Banwell, Somerset, 15th-century wooden rood-screen, showing cornice with bands of carving.

2. Ludham, Norfolk, rood-screen panels.

3. Happisburgh, Norfolk, another 15th-century wooden screen.

4. Compton Bassett, Wilts, stone screen.

Plate 36 1. All Saints', Hereford, stalls with canopies and misericords. 2. Flamborough, East Riding, rood-loft. 3. South Cerney, Glos, parts of medieval figure of Christ. 4. Attleborough, Norfolk, rood-loft.

land, Chaddesley Corbett, Worcs, Luppitt, Devon, Coleshill and Stoneleigh, Warwicks, Stottesdon, Salop, Hook Norton, Oxon, Thorpe Salvin, West Riding, and Reighton, East Riding.

At Burnham Deepdale, Norfolk, the Twelve Months are realistically carved, and at Fincham in the same county, figures well depict Old and New Testament episodes.

There are about thirty fonts made completely of lead. The majority are late Norman (Ashover, Derbyshire, Pl. 28, Dorchester Abbey, Oxon, and Brookland, Kent). There are seven richly ornamented Norman fonts of Tournai marble (East Meon,

13th-century font.
Leighton Buzzard, Beds.

14th-century font.
Brailes, Warwicks.

Hants). Norman fonts are usually circular or square.

A number of fonts were made in the Transitional period between Norman and Early English. The bowl is square and supported on a large central and four smaller corner shafts, the material often being Purbeck marble.

Early English fonts followed the style of the time in mouldings and ornament (Eaton Bray, Leighton Buzzard and Studham, Beds, and North Newbald, East Riding).

In the Decorated period an octagonal bowl is usual with niches which were then so popular on everything (Fishlake, West Riding, and Hitchin, Herts, each with figures occupying the niches). Sometimes the bowl is ornamented with tracery similar to that of the windows of the time (Brailes, Warwicks; a most interesting one of the same type but later is at Little Totham, Essex). A fine font with figures of saints, including St Christopher and St George, may be seen at Ware, Herts. Tysoe, Warwicks, also has figures of saints, and Shilton, Oxon, has carvings of Our Lord's Passion.

It is, however, in the fifteenth century, and in East Anglia, that the font reaches its highest development. It is frequently raised on steps which give it greater dignity. There are two main types:

(a) The stem is surrounded by lions and sometimes also by wild, hairy men with big clubs. The panels of the bowl are carved with the symbols of the four Evangelists alternating with angels holding musical instruments or shields. Sometimes lions take the place of the symbols of the Evangelists. This type in some such form is very common in Norfolk and Suffolk and is indeed most satisfying (Happisburgh, Surlingham, Pl. 29, Acle and

Upton, Norfolk, and Saxmundham and Chediston, Suffolk).

(b) Quite the most beautiful as well as the most interesting are those which show the Seven Sacraments of the Church on seven of the panels of the bowl and another subject (probably the Crucifixion or the Baptism of Our Lord) on the remaining panel. The Seven Sacraments are Baptism, Confirmation, Mass, Penance, Holy Orders, Holy Matrimony and Extreme Unction (which is the administration of the last Rites to the dying).

At Little Walsingham, Norfolk, and Laxfield, Suffolk, the steps themselves are works of art, but in every case the panels are worth detailed study as they show the costume of the period as well as vestments. The best preserved panels are at Gresham and Sloley (Pl. 28), Norfolk, and Badingham, Suffolk. Much original colour still remains at Great Witchingham, Norfolk, and Westhall, Suffolk. Walsoken, Norfolk (Pl. 27), has one of the most beautiful.

The order of the sacraments varies and each font depicts them in different ways. In all cases baptism is by immersion and confirmation is of infants (Sloley, Norfolk) (Pl. 28). In Penance at Westhall the devil is retreating, his tail between his legs.

The number of such Seven Sacrament fonts that remain, excluding a few completely defaced, are twenty-two in Norfolk and eleven in Suffolk. Very curiously only two exist elsewhere: they are at Farningham, Kent, and Nettlecombe, Somerset.

There are also two outstanding fonts of this period in Norfolk with sculpture of a different kind, namely at Stalham and Hemblington, the latter recently beautifully recoloured. Snape, Suffolk, must also receive special mention. Outside East Anglia there are fifteenth-century fonts with remarkably fine sculpture at Huttoft, Lincs, and at Shorne and Southfleet, Kent.

FONT COVERS

As the holy water, which had been blessed, remained in the font it was necessary that there should be a

Font covers.

Colebrooke,
Devon.

Monksilver,
Somerset.

locked cover. The marks of staples on some fonts today prove this, but numerous lovely wooden covers still remain.

Many churches might have been content with a flat cover, but often this was prolonged into an eight-sided cone. The eight angle ribs may be straight (Monksilver, Somerset), curved forming a hollow (Ashbocking, Suffolk), or of ogee form (Colebrooke, Devon). The cone might also surmount a drum (Banwell, Somerset) (Pl. 29). All these forms are found in medieval and post-Reformation work, the only clue to a date being the ornamentation—crockets and pinnacles in pre-Reformation times and Jacobean carving later, as at Rodney Stoke and Banwell, Somerset, Lanreath, Cornwall, and Astbury, Cheshire. Sometimes the ogee form was not boarded over, leaving eight radiating ogee trusses, as at Bolton Percy, West Riding.

In the medieval period in East Anglia, the simple drum with a number of pinnacles, as at Barking and Copdock, Suffolk, soon became the most splendid soaring mass of wonderful tabernacle work reaching almost to the roof. The finest example is at Ufford, Suffolk, and it is indeed the finest font cover in the world. It is crowned by a pelican. Amazing as it is, it would have been even more gorgeous with its colour and gilt.

Other similar covers can be seen at Castle Acre, Worstead and Sall, Norfolk, and St Gregory's, Sudbury, Worlingworth and Hepworth, Suffolk. There are also some examples in the north-east of England, as at Thirsk and Well (Pl. 29), North Riding.

Covers not lifted off by hand can be suspended from a beam in the roof, but there may be a font beam (Sheringham, Norfolk), or a bracket or crane, (Sall, Norfolk, and the remarkable coloured animal's head at Whaddon, Bucks).

The cover would be raised by means of a counterpoise. Most of the finest covers were telescopic with the counterpoise inside the upper part of the cover so that the lower portion of the cover telescopes over the upper portion. In other cases the counterpoise is outside the cover, as at Ewelme, Oxon, but it might be hidden by panelling, as at Pilton, Devon. In such cases the whole cover moved.

An amazing piece of medieval woodwork is the independent canopy standing on legs around the font at Trunch, Norfolk (Pl. 29). The actual cover (no longer remaining) telescoped into this canopy.

Occasionally the whole font was completely encased within its cover with doors giving access. A good example is at Swimbridge, Devon, which shows the early Renaissance carving typical of the West Country. Sometimes the inside of such covers has paintings (Terrington St Clement, Norfolk).

CHESTS

An old chest may sometimes be found, often also at the west end. In it were kept the valuables of the church. The earliest chests (sometimes possibly twelfth century) are of the crudest type known as "dug-outs": a great log was roughly squared, a slice sawn off the top to act as a lid, while the lower portion was hollowed out. (There are many in Warwickshire, as at Curdworth.)

A thirteenth-century chest often consisted of a great slab of wood flanked by two front uprights or stiles prolonged below the chest itself to raise it from the damp. Roundels of geometrical designs may occur on the central portion and stiles (Stoke D'Abernon, Surrey, and Earl Stonham, Suffolk). In the fourteenth century, heavy slabs of oak were

Chests.

Church Brampton,   Stoke D'Abernon,
Northants.   Surrey.

Selworthy,
Somerset.

clamped and bound with ironwork, either for strength in a number of bands (Selworthy, Somerset, and Warbleton, Sussex) or for ornament in elaborate scrollwork (Church Brampton, Northants, and Icklingham, Suffolk).

The most elaborate carving is on those 14th-century chests where the central portion and the stiles are treated differently; the stiles are divided into horizontal panels filled with carvings, dragons and grotesque figures, and the central portion has tracery (Wath, North Riding, and Saltwood, Kent), or even a tilting scene (Harty, Kent). The chest at Dersingham, Norfolk (Pl. 30), is carved with the symbols of the Four Evangelists with their names on labels. Splendid chests panelled throughout with tracery may be seen at Faversham, Kent, Huttoft, Lincs, and Crediton, Devon.

These old chests usually have at least three locks. Locks, bolts and hinges are often of the most ingenious construction. The ends of a chest sometimes have lifting rings for a chain or rope to be attached to a pole. Later chests follow the design of the period (Croscombe, Somerset—Jacobean).

Special mention must be made of the remarkable thirteenth-century chest at Newport, Essex. The inside of the cover is painted to form a reredos and the chest is therefore a portable altar. The paintings of the crucifixion and saints are the earliest English oil paintings on wood. There are five locks and a false bottom with a secret sliding panel which contained the altar stone.

WALL-PAINTINGS

Old churches were Bible picture books. Reading was altogether unknown save to the lettered few. Entering a church then must have been joyous, for surely the enjoyment must have been something like the pleasure derived from looking at one's favourite coloured slides or pictures. One must have felt transplanted to the Holy Land and really to be in the midst of the saints. The great truths of the

Gospel were indeed blazing forth in bright colours. Many incidents in Christ's life were shown, but the emphasis was, however, on the Nativity and the events of the Passion, thereby rightly stressing Our Lord's redemptive work.

Over the chancel arch (Pl. 36), or on boards filling up the arch, was almost invariably a painting of a Doom (or Last Judgment) which often formed a background to the great rood. (Good examples on boards, now moved down for inspection, can be seen at Wenhaston, Suffolk, Dauntsey, Wilts, and Penn, Bucks.) The usual arrangement was the figure of Christ Triumphant showing His wounds, seated in judgment, with heaven on one side and hell on the other, and probably St Michael with scales in between. (A demon is always trying to pull the scales down, but he is never successful.) The dead rise from their graves. The heavenly mansions look most uncomfortable. The medieval artist, however, enjoyed himself much more on the other side—hell. This is usually shown as the jaws of a large dragon with huge teeth and all enveloped in bright red flames. Demons with red-hot chains and pitchforks secure as many customers as possible. The church of St Thomas, Salisbury (Pl. 30), has a good, though restored, example. Other examples are the Guild Chapel, Stratford-on-Avon, Patcham, Sussex, and Combe, North Leigh and South Leigh, Oxon. St Michael weighing souls can be found at South Leigh (restored) and Swalcliffe, Oxon.

The most popular single subject on walls was St Christopher carrying the infant Christ across the river. He is almost invariably depicted opposite the principal entrance. It was thought that whoever looked upon such a figure would be free from sudden death that day (and would thus have an opportunity for repentance). St Christopher is, of course, the patron saint of travellers. The saint has a long flowering staff, and the Child carries an orb (representing the world) surmounted by a cross. A hermit with a lantern is usually shown and in the river may be fish and ships. Examples are common in East Anglia, mostly of the fifteenth century. Hayes, Middx, Horley, Oxon, Little Baddow, Essex, Baunton, Glos, Ridge, Herts, Oaksey, Wilts, Edingthorpe and Hardley, Norfolk, and Little Missenden, Bucks, are fine. Two, very brightly restored, can be seen at Poughill, near Bude, Cornwall. Breage (Pl. 30) is another example in the same county. Only two churches have paintings of various scenes from his life: Shorwell, Isle of Wight, and Hemblington, Norfolk.

St George and the dragon come next in popularity (St Gregory's, Norwich, Dartford, Kent, and Broughton, Bucks), and then St Catherine and St Margaret. Another popular subject was The Three Living and The Three Dead, a morality picture on the vanity of life—three richly robed kings hunting and three skeleton kings reminding them of their end (Raunds, Northants).

Even more popular are the Seven Deadly Sins—they always have been! Their representation in wall-paintings is very interesting (again at Raunds). Pride is the root of all the other sins. It is usually shown as a human figure or as a tree rising from hell, scrolls proceeding to six dragons' jaws in which are shown the remaining sins—anger, envy, sloth, avarice, gluttony and lust. By contrast, the Seven Works of Mercy may appear, as at Trotton, Sussex. (These are feeding the hungry, giving drink to the thirsty, clothing the naked, housing the stranger, visiting the sick, comforting the prisoners and burying the dead.) It would not be a bad idea for every church to have such pictures today.

Christ blessing Trades, shown by various implements, agricultural and mining, is particularly popular in Cornwall (Breage) (Pl. 30).

The walls of the little church of Hardham, Sussex, are covered with paintings of 1100. Not much later are those at Kempley, Glos, Clayton, Sussex, and Copford, Essex (restored). One remarkable painting of 1200 must be mentioned. It is the Ladder of Salvation and it covers the whole of the west wall of Chaldon, Surrey. The subject is common in the Eastern Church, but this is the only one in England. Sutton Bingham, Somerset (Pl. 30), has a superb painting of the Coronation of the Virgin of about 1300.

For a small country church, quite unrestored and covered with wall-paintings, one cannot do better than visit Tarrant Crawford, Dorset. Chalgrove, Oxon, and Croughton, Northants, are also notable. The most complete series, however, though restored, is at Pickering, North Riding.

Real artists were involved, for these paintings are usually great works of art—what could surpass in beauty the figures of Our Lady and Child of about 1250 at Great Canfield, Essex?

Many medieval paintings must still be covered up and unknown. This is therefore the one field left in which exciting discoveries can be made.

BENCHES

Wooden benches of the thirteenth century exist (Dunsfold, Surrey) and numbers of fifteenth-century date remain, proving that seating was usual before the Reformation. Before the fifteenth century, however, it is possible that the only seating was sometimes a stone bench around the walls or piers. It must, of course, be remembered that the worship of the medieval Church did not require much in the way of seating. At a plain service of Holy Communion today one does not sit at all, and when the service is sung, one sits only for the reading of the Epistle and during the sermon.

In East Anglia the tops of the ends of the benches nearly always take the most fascinating form known as a poppy-head (probably derived from puppis, the figure-head of a ship). Below the poppy-heads are usually carvings of human figures or animals which sometimes surmount small buttresses at the sides of the standards or ends. The ends are sometimes panelled; the backs are often pierced with delicate tracery. The finest examples are at Wiggenhall St Mary the Virgin (Pl. 31) and Wiggenhall St Germans, Norfolk. The church best filled with such old benches is, however, at Fressingfield, Suffolk. Several churches, such as Woolpit, Dennington, Ufford and Stowlangtoft, Suffolk, and Harpley and Great Walsingham, Norfolk (Pl. 31), are also well filled.

Bench-end; Sloth.
Blythburgh, Suffolk.

Bench-end.
Combs, Suffolk

Interesting bench-ends can be seen in the churches of Ixworth Thorpe, Wordwell, Wilby, Athelington and Tannington, Suffolk. Some poppy-heads at Blythburgh, Suffolk, are realistically carved with the Seven Deadly Sins: sloth is always a favourite! There is an ingenious poppy-head of three fishes at Stanground, Hunts. A church with poppy-head benches cannot be surpassed for beauty anywhere so far as its seating is concerned.

The west of England is also profusely supplied with old benches, but here the ends are nearly always square-headed; figure carving (often secular and of an early Renaissance type) and foliage are common. The fronts and backs of a block of benches often have the same rich carving. In a splendid group around the Quantock Hills, Somerset, the ends are carved with much foliage and traceried panelling (Monksilver, Broomfield, Crowcombe, Milverton, Spaxton and Bishop's Hull). Barwick, Somerset, also has some interesting bench-ends.

In Devon (old benches are more profuse in the north of the county than in the south) and Cornwall the old bench-ends often have heraldic devices. Cornwall has a wealth of old seating and here carved Instruments of the Passion (p. 188) are particularly popular; the example illustrated (Pl. 31) is from Braunton, Devon. In these two counties the edges of the ends have scrolls of foliage, usually long, pointed leaves with indented edges. Churches in which the original seating is fairly complete are East Budleigh, Braunton (Pl. 31), Lapford, Abbotsham, High Bickington and Lew Trenchard, Devon, and Kilkhampton, Launcells, Altarnun (Pl. 44), Lanteglos-by-Fowey (Pl. 1), Talland, Lansallos, Mullion and St Winnow, Cornwall.

Some bench-ends at Combe-in-Teignhead, Devon, have delightful figures. Five bench-ends at Trull, Somerset, must also be mentioned. They show figures in a religious procession—very remarkable for so late a date as 1560. Three bench-ends at Brent Knoll, Somerset, depict the humorous animal fable of Reynard the Fox, who is disguised as a mitred abbot. Pl. 31 shows him with birds and three monks in cowls who have heads of swine; at the foot two

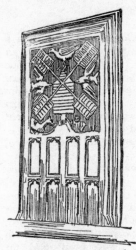

Cartouche tablet.
King's Caple,
Herefords.

Windmill bench-end.
Bishop's Lydeard, Somerset.

monkeys roast a pig on a spit, and above is a chained
ape with a money bag. Windmills occur on bench-
ends at Bishop's Lydeard (with miller) and North
Cadbury, Somerset, and Thornham, Norfolk.

In the Midlands medieval bench-ends were normally square-headed and quite plain (Minster Lovell,
Oxon), but sometimes with small buttresses.

Linen-fold panelling was often used in Tudor
times, and bench-ends of that date sometimes have
it; it is as if a piece of linen is laid in vertical folds
(p. 120).

Box-pews are referred to on page 121.

LECTERNS

In medieval times the Gospel was read from a lectern in the chancel. It was usually of metal or wood and movable, more rarely fixed and of stone protruding from the north wall of the chancel near the High Altar, as can be seen in several Derbyshire churches (Etwall). After the Reformation the lectern was moved into the nave and from it are read the Lessons at Matins and Evensong.

The movable lecterns, whether of metal or wood, are of two forms:

(a) A simple desk, single, two-sided, or four-sided, supported on a pillar. Splendid examples of wood are at Detling, Kent (Pl. 32), Shipdham, Norfolk, and Bury, Hunts, and of metal at Yeovil, Somerset, and in the chapels of Merton College, Oxford, and Eton College. This type, particularly those with two or more sides, would have been used for supporting the large music books then used for antiphonal singing, and the desk at Ranworth, Norfolk, has music painted upon its upper desk (and an eagle on its lower desk).

(b) An eagle, or very occasionally a pelican, supporting the book on its outstretched wings These are often of the fifteenth or sixteenth centuries. Old brass eagle lecterns are lovely works of art. Three animals at the base are usual, as if guarding the book above. Just over forty remain (Wolborough and Bovey Tracey, Devon, Oundle, Northants, Isleham, Cambs, Pl. 32, and Clare, Suffolk). Of old wooden eagles about twenty still exist (Astbury, Cheshire, Pl. 32, and Ottery St Mary,

Devon). The popularity of the form of an eagle is thought to be because it is the symbol of St John the Evangelist, whose Gospel and Revelation are the most spiritual part of the Bible, and, like the eagle, soar to the greatest heights.

PULPITS

One can nearly always recognize pre-Reformation work by its perfect proportions. This certainly applies to pulpits. At that time they were tall and narrow and usually supported on a long slender stem. Many of the Victorian period are the reverse and therefore quite out of place in a country church.

About one hundred of wood remain from before the Reformation and they are most numerous in Norfolk and Devon. In the former county panels painted with figures of saints, as on screens, were popular. A perfect and unrestored example of about 1475 remains at Burnham Norton (Pl. 33), showing the Four Latin Doctors (p. 189). Figure paintings can also be seen at Castle Acre and Horsham St Faith. South Burlingham has an equally lovely coloured pulpit, but with foliage instead of figures. In Devon, the rich and massive foliage of the area and niches are popular, and when the colouring remains the sight is gorgeous. We can mention Halberton, Kenton, Ipplepen, Coleridge, East Allington, Holne and Chivelstone (hollowed out of a single block of oak and with much original colour remaining).

One of the most beautiful of wood is, however, at Long Sutton in Somerset, and is a good example of

Linen-fold panelling.
Onibury, Salop.

Three-decker pulpit.
Cottesbrooke, Northants.

colour. It has sixteen sides and figures of the Twelve
Apostles, but these are new. Nor must we overlook
Trull, in the same county. It has its original carved
figures of the Four Latin Doctors and St John the
Evangelist. (These figures are said to have been
buried and hence their preservation.)

Medieval pulpits of stone number about sixty and
they are most common in Somerset, Gloucestershire and Devon. In the first-named county, the
fine church of Banwell (Pl. 33) has one that is

similar to about fifteen in that delightful area. Northleach is an example from the second county, and in Devon we again have the luxuriant foliage and niches, as at St Saviour's, Dartmouth, Bovey Tracey, Dittisham (Pl. 2) and Harberton—all with colour and most remarkable; others with figures exist at South Molton, Swimbridge, Chittlehampton and Witheridge. The most notable stone pulpit, with staircase, is, however, at St Peter's, Wolverhampton.

In the late sixteenth and early seventeenth centuries the chief features of interest added to a church were pulpits and monuments. A great number of wooden pulpits were constructed and are generally termed Jacobean. They are exceedingly pleasing in design. Round-arched arcading is prominent on all woodwork of the period (Bishop's Lydeard, Somerset) (Pl. 33). Very often above the pulpit is a large sounding-board or tester supported on a standard or backpiece. Grand examples can be found at Lenham, Kent, Newport, Isle of Wight, Stoke D'Abernon, Surrey, Ivinghoe and Cheddington, Bucks, Brancepeth, County Durham, Croscombe, Somerset, Cerne Abbas and Abbotsbury, Dorset, Brinkworth, Wilts, and Burgh-le-Marsh, Lincs.

Stoke St Gregory has a quaint figure of Father Time (no doubt very appropriate when everyone is looking at the pulpit during the sermon!) (Pl. 33).

In the late seventeenth and early eighteenth centuries "three-deckers" became the fashion. They are prayer-desk, lectern and pulpit combined in one, but at different heights. High box-pews usually accompanied them. Six well-known examples of medieval churches with these additions (and without any Victorian restoration removing them) are Whitby, North Riding, Teversal, Notts, Minstead, Hants, Old Dilton, Wilts, and Parracombe and Molland (Pl. 32), Devon. Stanstead Abbots, Herts, still retains its box-pews and "three-decker", and a delightful small ancient church complete with eighteenth-century fittings is at Winterborne Tomson, Dorset. (Complete churches of this period are mentioned on p. 99.)

The real delight of an old church is often its quaintness with odd bits and pieces. Cameley and Puxton (Pl. 44), Somerset, Inglesham, Wilts, Old Romney, Kent, and Onibury, Salop, are a few amongst many which fortunately remain.

Another particular charm of a country church is its smell. Only centuries, and no doubt a little damp, can produce it.

HOUR-GLASSES

These were introduced in the later sixteenth century for regulating the length of the sermon (and are exactly the same as the present-day egg timer, but larger). About 120 stands and some glasses remain. They varied in length of time, but the maximum was made for an hour. One could imagine the congregation when it was turned over for "another glass".

The usual method was to attach an iron bracket to the pulpit, or occasionally to the adjacent wall. Most brackets were very simple, but sometimes there was considerable skill in ironwork. Hurst and Binfield, Berks, are exceptionally elaborate. There are two very curious examples in neighbouring churches,

Pilton and Tawstock (Pl. 34), Devon, where the bracket of sheet-iron is in the form of an arm holding the glass in the hand. At Earl Stonham, Suffolk, there are no less than four glasses.

READING DESKS

Double reading desks at the east end of the nave are now rare. A handsome Jacobean one is at Cumnor, Berks.

ENTRANCE TO THE CHANCEL

The entrance to the chancel was always important. Confirmation and Marriage are conducted there. In medieval times the body of the church, the nave, was used for many secular purposes as it was then probably the only public place of meeting in the village. It was therefore usual to erect a screen dividing the nave from the chancel which was the more holy part of the church in which was the Sacramental presence (much as in a dual-purpose church today). It also defined the boundary between nave and chancel, the parishioners being responsible for the repair of the former (with the screen) and the rector (possibly a lay rector) for that of the latter. This is why the two parts so often differ in size and date.

ROOD-SCREENS

Devon is noted for its magnificent fifteenth-century wooden screens and most are still coloured and gilt (Wolborough). The panels at the base usually have numerous painted figures, the tracery is bold and follows the local Perpendicular window tracery, the fan vaulting is massive, and the cornice has several bands of wonderful carving (Banwell, Somerset) (Pl. 35). The figure paintings are more stumpy than in East Anglia and of less artistic merit, but nevertheless are of the greatest possible interest; the delightful village of Ashton has the best, Pl. 34, showing St Sitha and St Michael, and there is an even more remarkable series of prophets on the backs of the panels. These screens usually stretch from one side of the church to the other in one unbroken line. Many fortunately remain. It is difficult to make any choice, but we mention Bovey Tracey, Bradninch, Chulmleigh, Cullompton, St Saviour's, Dartmouth, Hartland, Kentisbeare, Lapford (Pl. 34) and Plymtree. (Similar fine ones in Somerset are at Dunster, Minehead, Carhampton and Banwell.) (Pl. 35).

The fifteenth-century wooden screens of East Anglia are quite different, being higher and lighter than the Devon examples. The distinguishing feature is a bold crocketed hood-mould, usually of ogee form, applied to delicate tracery (Happisburgh, Pl. 34, and Scarning, Norfolk). Many of the screens were square-headed, that is to say, without a vault, and if vaulted the vault is not so massive as in Devon, but it may be of a rich pendant type giving complete bays (Bramfield, Suffolk) (Pl. 34). The tracery also is not so conspicuous and sometimes, particularly if there is a vault, there is no tracery at all, but merely plain openings relieved by a few cusps. Beautiful vaulted screens remain at Attleborough, Norfolk (Pl. 36), and Bramfield, Suffolk (Pl. 34).

Good examples of fourteenth-century screens are at Thompson, Norfolk, and Fritton, Suffolk (Pl. 20). It was, however, in the fifteenth century in East Anglia that the wood-carver really came into his own with the collaboration of the painter who added all colours, particularly red, green and gold, so that these screens became priceless works of art of sheer beauty unrivalled anywhere.

The panels at the base often have a variety of designs in the spandrels—flowers, beasts, birds and grotesques (Suffield, Norfolk). The backgrounds are alternately red and green (costumes of figures also usually counter-changing). Nothing is more delightful than the figure paintings. The Twelve Apostles are the favourite subject in East Anglia, but angels and archangels, prophets, martyrs, kings, archbishops, bishops, deacons and the Four Latin Doctors may be found in different churches and their identification is a fascinating task (St Catherine with her wheel, for example). Truth and legend are equally well represented. Many of the saints are obscure, but they probably had a dramatic death or were useful patron saints, such as St Apollonia, the patron saint of sufferers from toothache. Churches having beautiful painted screen panels are at Barton Turf, Ludham (Pl. 35), Cawston, Beeston Regis (Pl. 3), Hunstanton and Carleton Rode in Norfolk, and Southwold (Pl. 2), Eye, Westhall and Somerleyton in Suffolk. At Southwold (Pl. 2), Bramfield and on some other Suffolk screens the background is rich gesso work (gold). The finest screen is at Ranworth, Norfolk; it has parclose screens (side screens) to enclose the nave altars, the wooden reredoses to which are also part of the screen, the whole being adorned with figures considered to be the finest in the whole country. Barton Turf has a notable series of paintings of the Nine Orders of Angels. The screen panels at Wellingham, Norfolk, are of a rare type with scenes showing the Resurrection, St Michael and St George.

The Midland screens are much plainer and are not of such a distinctive type, and figure painting in the lower panels is very rare; Handborough, Oxon, is typical. Not far away, at Charlton-on-Otmoor, Oxon, the screen has linen-fold panels and shows Brittany influence in its shafts with honeycomb patterns. Cheshire has some fine screens, as at Astbury and Mobberley.

The earliest complete rood-screen is of thirteenth-century date in the interesting church of Stanton Harcourt, Oxon.

Old screens of stone are comparatively rare. In parish churches they normally followed the design of the wood-carver and there are several in Wiltshire (Hilmarton and Compton Bassett, Pl. 35). Totnes, Devon, has one of the finest. There are two in Essex at Stebbing and Great Bardfield which are of a unique design with rood combined.

In the Jacobean period wooden screens are ornamented with round-arched arcading and strap-work ornament (a geometrical pattern of interlacing straps, p. 53) and obelisks on the cornice. They were rarely necessary as chancel screens, as churches usually possessed one already, but Croscombe and Rodney Stoke, Somerset, are examples. Screens at this time therefore more often formed side screens

(Yarnton, Oxon), or screens to ante-chapels and halls in Oxford and Cambridge colleges. County Durham has some notable seventeenth-century woodwork, as at Brancepeth and Sedgefield.

ROOD-LOFTS

The loft or platform above a screen was supported on (a) a vault, (b) a deep cove or concave arch, or (c) the floor would rest upon the top bar of the screen and on a beam placed parallel to it and about two feet in advance of it. This gallery was protected front and back by panelling. Only about a dozen old rood-loft fronts remain in the whole of England, but there are several in Wales. It was one of the first parts of a church to be destroyed at the Reformation with the great crucifix above it.

One of the main uses of the rood-loft was accommodation for the choir, instrumentalists, and organ (if any). The Gospel was not read from it, except perhaps in collegiate churches. Many churches still have the staircase in a wall or turret (Burrington, Somerset) by which the rood-loft was reached (sometimes with the original doors; see p. 55).

Two magnificent rood-lofts remain: one is at Attleborough, Norfolk (Pl. 36), upon the front of which after the Reformation were painted the Arms of the old dioceses of England and Wales; the other is at Flamborough, East Riding (Pl. 36), with all its niches complete, but the figures are missing. If one can imagine such a loft front in its glory, with figures, gilt and colouring, one can visualize a little the magnificence of a church just before the Reformation.

On top of the rood-loft front or on a separate beam above it was the great rood or crucifix. This is why these screens are called rood-screens. On either side of the cross would have been figures of St Mary the Virgin and St John the Evangelist. Behind this group of figures was usually the Doom painting, as has been mentioned (p. 111), and often these paintings show the unpainted spaces against which were placed the great cross and the figures (Raunds, Northants).

It was most appropriate that such a group should be at the entrance to the chancel. The crucifix was then the most prominent object and dominated the nave in the later medieval period; walls were heightened, clerestories added, or additional windows inserted in order to set off and give prominence to this representation of the greatest Fact in history, showing that mankind had not been left to struggle alone, but had been redeemed by Christ on the Cross. The Passion of Our Lord and the shadow of the Cross were very properly the predominant thoughts of a medieval Christian.

There is little doubt that almost every old church would have had some such screen and loft—many no doubt very simple.

Above the rood was often a canopy of honour called a rood celure, usually formed by panelling or by colouring and enriching the eastern bay of the nave roof (King's Nympton and Ideford, Devon, Stowlangtoft, Suffolk, Pl. 23, and Braughing, Herts).

After the Reformation the figures were destroyed. Only two churches retain parts of the figure of Christ: South Cerney, Glos (Pl. 36), now in Cardiff Museum, and Cartmel Fell, Lancs. The Doom painting was then frequently whitewashed and its place taken by the Royal Arms, Lord's Prayer, Creed and Ten Commandments. A remarkable example of 1587 is at Tivetshall St Margaret, Norfolk.

Large paintings of Moses and Aaron also then became popular, as at Marton, Cheshire.

The screen at Eye, Suffolk, has been splendidly restored, with rood and loft complete with colouring, and gives an excellent idea of the appearance of a medieval screen in all its grandeur.

STALLS

The chancels of most churches had wooden stalls which would be placed against the north and south walls and are often "returned", or set, against the back of the screen, that is, three or four on each side of the entrance facing eastwards. Parish churches never had more than one row. In the greater churches there were marvellous tabernacled canopies, but small churches at the most had traceried backs and cornice. The elbows might be adorned with angels whose wings follow the curve, the fronts of the desks usually have traceried heads (Sall, Norfolk) and the ends are often poppy-heads.

Stalls in parish churches with wonderful tabernacled canopies can be seen at Lancaster, Beverley Minster, East Riding, and Nantwich, Cheshire. All Saints', Hereford (Pl. 36) has good examples.

Traceried backs are well seen at Tong, Salop, and the stall backs at Cartmel Priory, Lancs, are notable for Renaissance carving of the early seventeenth century.

It would appear that the stalls in a parish church were originally provided for the parish priest, parish clerk, any chaplains or chantry priests, and for the patron and leading churchfolk. Only in the nineteenth century was it the custom for a choir of men and boys to be installed in the chancel, and modern stalls were often erected for the purpose. Removal of this modern work in old churches opens up the chancel to its original medieval beauty.

MISERICORDS

Tip-up seats in stalls are called misericords and underneath them are projections which when turned up afford some support when one is standing, and one's elbows can rest on the arms of the stalls (Pl. 36).

On either side of the main projection or centre-piece are nearly always subsidiary carvings known as supporters, which are generally different in design and subject from the centre-piece—often human heads, animals or foliage. The carvings can be appreciated by anyone, but their meaning will only be understood by very few who have learnt their "language". Here we can only recommend detailed study of the subjects and their meaning which will be most rewarding. Inspiration was obtained from the *Biblia Pauperum*, a picture-book of the Scriptures of about 1300, from the *Speculum Humanae Salvationis* on secular history and legends, and even more from the *Bestiary*, a book on animals.

Symbolism by type and anti-type was most popular. For instance, Samson carrying off the gates of Gaza, as at Ripon Minster, is associated with the Resurrection. The pelican in her piety is very common (Lavenham, Suffolk); the bird pecks its breast and gives its blood to its young ones, as Christ redeemed us by His blood and still gives it to us. There are numerous fine owls (Norwich Cathedral): they were not then thought to be wise, but the opposite—very foolish. They preferred darkness to light and symbolized the Jews who were blind to the new daylight of Christianity.

In addition to birds, beasts and fishes, the principal subjects covered were mythology, medieval romances (such as Reynard the Fox and the Romance of Alexander), homely domestic life, sport, jesters, heraldry and satires—particularly on monks, doctors and musicians. The occupations of the twelve months are realistically carved at Ripple, Worcs. (Pl. 37 is of reaping in August.) Sacred subjects are comparatively rare.

We now give two examples of their meaning. A king between two griffins, as at Wells Cathedral, represents the flight of Alexander the Great, who, thinking that he was at the end of the world, wanted to see what was beyond it, and so ascended to a height in a basket between two powerful birds—so perhaps he was the first spaceman!

Our other example can be seen on misericords at Westminster Abbey and Worcester Cathedral, and it is the Judgment of Solomon. The king is seen with two mothers, one holding a large and vigorous kicking baby, the other a small dead baby in swaddling clothes. One infant died and its mother secretly changed it for the living one. A dispute ensued and the king was asked to settle it. He asked for a sword and stated that he would cut the live child in half for each mother, whereupon the real mother of the live one at once cried out that the other could have the whole child, the other insisting upon a division. The true ownership was then quite clear.

Humour and wise saws can also be found. At Beverley Minster, East Riding, a man is shoeing a goose, which is based on the saying that if you meddle in something that you do not understand, you might as well try to shoe a goose.

Vast numbers of misericords of various dates remain, especially in the greater churches. There are large numbers in the cathedrals of Lincoln, Norwich, Wells, Ely, Exeter and Worcester, as well as in the chapels of New College, Oxford, and King's College, Cambridge, St George's Chapel, Windsor, and Henry VII's Chapel, Westminster Abbey. Some misericords in the North are unsurpassed for their carving, namely those in Ripon, Chester, Manchester and Carlisle cathedrals. In parish churches there are 32 at Ludlow, Salop, and double that number at Boston, Lincs. At Beverley, East Riding, there are 68 in the Minster and 28 in the almost equally fine church of St Mary (p. 208).

HATCHMENTS

A coat of Arms on a lozenge-shaped frame is a

hatchment. It was hung for some months in front of the house of a deceased person and then brought into the church. Many churches possess quite a number. There are seventeen in the exceptionally interesting church of Stanford, Northants. They are usually late seventeenth or eighteenth century in date. The word "Resurgam" often occurs. It is not a motto but a usual statement of belief, "I will rise again." Our illustration (Pl. 37) is from the church of Hoveton St Peter, Norfolk.

The background is either completely black or half black and half white according to the married state of the deceased. These are the rules:

Black background
>   Bachelor—Arms are single (i.e. just his family).
>   Widower—Arms are divided into two (i.e. husband's and wife's Arms).
>   Spinster—Arms are single and lozenge-shaped.
>   Widow—Arms are divided into two and lozenge-shaped.

Half black and half white backgrounds
>   Married man dies before wife—left side (as you look at it) black and right side white.
>   Married woman dies before husband—left side white and right side black.

ROYAL ARMS

The Royal Arms are usually painted on a square board or on canvas, but sometimes they are carved in plaster, stone or wood. Such Royal Arms are not earlier than Henry VIII (a fine example being at Rushbrooke, Suffolk), but they became general in the reign of Elizabeth I (Kenninghall and Tivetshall St Margaret, Norfolk) (see page 129).

After the Restoration they became compulsory in churches and the Arms of Charles II are therefore common, particularly in the West Country. In the reign of George I, the earlier Arms of Charles were sometimes brought up to date by making the initial C into a G and other amendments.

From earliest times Royal Arms can be useful clues to dates in old churches. This is a summary (quarters being numbered   1   2
                                    3   4):

Before 1340   3 gold lions on red.

1340 to 1405   1 and 4 France, many gold fleurs-de-lys on blue.
2 and 3 England, 3 gold lions on red.

1405 to 1603   As before, but the fleurs-de-lys are now only three in number.

1603 to 1707   1 and 4 England and France quarterly as in the previous period.
2 Scotland, red lion and border on gold.
3 Ireland, gold harp on blue.

(Lydiard Tregoze, Wilts, Pl. 37, has Royal Arms of this period.)

(From 1689 to 1702 William and Mary added a gold lion on blue in the centre.)

1707 to 1714   1 and 4 England impaling Scotland.
2 3 fleurs-de-lys of France.
3 harp of Ireland.

1714 to 1801   As previously, but with the Arms of Hanover in the fourth quarter

1801 to 1837   1 and 4 England, 2 Scotland, 3 Ireland, and the Arms of Hanover in the centre.

1837 to the   As in the previous period but without present time the centrepiece.

James I substituted the unicorn as a supporter with the lion in place of the Welsh dragon, which had been adopted by the Tudor sovereigns. Edward VI had replaced a greyhound with the lion. Supporters are figures on each side of a coat of Arms.

PRE-REFORMATION MONUMENTS

Even if a church appears to be rebuilt and uninteresting, it may well have monuments of great interest from its medieval predecessor. Monuments show the personal element in the parish and the various fashions through the ages.

Many medieval monuments with effigies remain in all parts of the country. The material was alabaster (which was our English marble and came from Chellaston, Derbyshire, Nottingham being an important centre for its manufacture), stone (including much Purbeck marble earlier in the period), or very occasionally wood (all would have been coloured). The most costly material, however, was bronze, and the royal monuments in Westminster Abbey are magnificent examples. There are, indeed, only two others of that material in England, namely at Canterbury Cathedral (the Black Prince) and at St Mary's, Warwick (Richard Beauchamp, perhaps the most sumptuous effigy in the whole country).

Many pre-Reformation monuments were surmounted by a canopy, which was often elaborately treated, and possibly vaulted. Examples of canopies are: thirteenth century, Edmund Crouchback, Westminster Abbey; fourteenth century, the Percy monument in Beverley Minster, East Riding (Pl. 40) (or, more simply, in many village churches, as at Winchelsea, Sussex); fifteenth century, Ewelme, Oxon. The last is the monument to the Duchess of Suffolk (1475), which can possibly claim to be the finest monument in England. She wears the Order of the Garter. Under her figure is a cadaver, a feature which became common in the fifteenth century. The church of Ewelme and the old fifteenth-century red brick almshouses and school make a charming picture.

Often around the sides of a medieval tomb are delightful little figures called weepers; they might be members of the family, angels or saints. Angels are either feathered or in albs and they often hold shields. The Ewelme monument is a good example. The beautiful monument at Chillingham, Northumberland (Pl. 38), to Sir Ralph Gray, 1443, has saints and angels.

Earlier in the fifteenth century are the two splendid figures of Ralph Greene and his wife (1419) hand in hand at Lowick, Northants. Sir Samson de Strelley and his wife of about 1400 at Strelley, Notts (Pl. 38), are likewise hand in hand. The monument to Sir Edmund de Thorpe and his wife, slightly later, at Ashwellthorpe, Norfolk (Pl. 38), is also very fine.

A good example of effigies of the fourteenth

century is again at St Mary's, Warwick (Thomas Beauchamp). Earlier in that century and at the end of the previous century many figures have crossed legs and have a life-like appearance as if alert and about to rise (Dorchester Abbey, Oxon, Pl. 37, and Whatton, Notts).

In the early thirteenth century and earlier, tapering grave-covers of stone were the most usual type of monument. They were usually decorated with a cross (Studley, Warwicks). Numbers remain, not, of course, always in their original positions, and they may be the oldest part of the church.

In the fifteenth and sixteenth centuries, the figures of the deceased and the family were sometimes incised in the stone or alabaster; this is common in the north Midlands, as at Pitchford, Salop, where the church adjoins the fine black-and-white Hall, and where there are four such slabs, one with twenty children. Engravings on slate are frequent in Cornwall (Lelant).

Medieval monuments can be well studied at Tong, Salop, Elford, Staffs, Much Marcle, Herefords, Stanton Harcourt, Oxon, and Ashbourne and Norbury, Derbyshire.

Diminutive monuments (sometimes connected with a heart burial) are always very charming, as at Youlgreave, Derbyshire, and Haccombe, Devon.

Only about eighty old wooden effigies still exist, most being in Essex. A good example of the fifteenth century is at Wingfield, Suffolk, and of the sixteenth century at Slindon, Sussex (Pl. 39).

Throughout the medieval period and later one can date an effigy or a brass by the armour of a knight, the dress and hair of a civilian, or a lady's dress and head-dress. Medieval carved figures, with only one or two exceptions, are in humble recumbent attitudes, with hands folded in prayer.

Sometimes a medieval monument was surrounded by an iron railing (Farleigh Hungerford, Somerset), such occasionally having little prickets or spikes for candles (West Tanfield, North Riding).

CHANTRY CHAPELS

A predominant feature of the fifteenth and early sixteenth centuries was the erection of chantry chapels and guild chapels, either within the church surrounded by a screen, or as an addition to the main structure. They contained the altar at which Mass would frequently be said for the repose of the souls of the founders and their relatives, or of the members of the guilds. Guilds were then popular and were associations for the welfare of their members and for the regulation of their trade. Burford, Oxon, has both types—a small structure within the church and an additional chapel. Winchester Cathedral has examples of the former, and lovely ones in parish churches are at Tewkesbury Abbey, Glos, Newark, Notts, Christchurch Priory, Hants, and Boxgrove Priory, Sussex.

The Kirkham chantry screen at Paignton, Devon (Pl. 40), with a panel depicting the Mass of St Gregory, is sumptuous.

Ely Cathedral chantries are additional chapels, but the most gorgeous is the Beauchamp Chapel,

Warwick. Henry VII's Chapel, Westminster Abbey, is, of course, a chantry chapel.

Additional aisles built for the purpose, showing Perpendicular at its best, are at Bromham and St John's, Devizes, Wilts, North Leigh, Oxon, and Tiverton and Cullompton, Devon.

TUDOR MONUMENTS

Great families and rich merchants increased in numbers in Tudor times and often wished to be commemorated by sumptuous monuments. After the Reformation, with the change of religious ideas, the attitude of the figures on monuments changed as well, and a variety of undevotional attitudes were adopted, the favourite being that of lolling on the elbow. The recumbent attitude, of course, continued as well in the sixteenth and seventeenth centuries, and many figures are shown kneeling. Needless to say all attitudes can sometimes be seen on the same monument.

Framlingham, Suffolk, is noted for its Tudor monuments to the Howards. Other notable examples of the period are at Brington (Spencer family) and Fawsley (Knightley family), Northants. The monument to Lord Marney at Layer Marney, Essex, is of terra-cotta and combines Gothic and Renaissance details. Sir Alexander Culpeper and his wife, 1537, at Goudhurst, Kent, are of wood and are remarkable for their colour and the ornamentation on his armour.

Tudor and seventeenth-century monuments together can be well studied in the churches of Bottesford, Leics, Exton, Rutland, and St Helen's, Bishopsgate, in the City of London. There are several splendid ones at Brewood, Staffs, with nearly fifty children—thirteen out of eighteen on one monument being shown in chrysom robes. (A chrysom is a robe confined in long swaddling bands and was worn by an infant after baptism until the churching of the mother, babies being then baptized when only a few days old.)

The monument to Sir Roger Manwood, 1592, in St Stephen's, Canterbury, shows him in life as a half-length figure or bust, but on the ledge below is a "life-like" full-length skeleton.

A most splendid example of the lolling attitude is at Swinbrook, Oxon (Pls. 39 and 41); two adjoining monuments produce six such figures in tiers of three (members of the great family of Fettiplace).

SEVENTEENTH-CENTURY MONUMENTS

Those of the first quarter of this century, generally termed Jacobean, are of the greatest possible interest and beauty. They are usually of immense size, lavishly coloured, and adorned with innumerable shields with coats of Arms. The crests at the heads of the figures and the animals at their feet are usually works of art in themselves. The armour and costume of this period are very striking. Round the sides all the children are "kneeling in relief" as guide books put it, as if the relief referred to is the death of the parents! With the numbers of children then involved, boys take up one side and girls another side. A skull held by a child indicates that he or she had previously died.

It is not generally realized how many such monuments there are. In a day's visiting of churches, one church at least is likely to provide a good example, and in view of the wide choice it is difficult to select a few to mention in this book:

Tawstock, Devon (Bourchier family) (the Saracen's head, goat and kneeling figures are particularly attractive); Bisham, Berks (Pl. 4) (three Hoby monuments, one with a red heart and life-like swans); Wellington, Somerset (Pl. 38) (Lord Chief Justice Popham with no less than twenty-eight figures); Rotherfield Greys, Oxon (Sir Francis Knollys, wearing the mantle of the Order of the Garter, with a perfectly charming infant at the side of the mother; in addition to the fourteen children round the sides, the eldest son and his wife kneel at a prayer desk on top of the monument); Harefield, Middx (Countess of Derby); Gawsworth, Cheshire (the Fittons, but apart from the monuments, the church should be visited because of its delightful situation adjoining the marvellous black-and-white half-timbered Hall and Old Rectory); Stoke D'Abernon (Vincent family) and Cheam (the Lumley Chapel), Surrey; Wickhamford, Worcs (Sandys family); Langar, Notts (Scroope family); Easton Neston, Northants (the Fermor monument with sixteen pennons arranged in the form of a peacock's tail); and Musbury, Devon (Drake family).

Slightly later in the century are two monuments which are particularly noteworthy and somewhat similar. One is by Nicholas Stone at Bramfield, Suffolk. It is to Arthur Coke and his wife, the latter holding a small infant; the wife and baby make the effigy one of the most wonderful achievements of

English sculpture. The other is the Savage monument at Elmley Castle, Worcs (Pl. 39); the baby is again a masterpiece. There is another babe in its mother's arms in Worcestershire, at Croome D'Abitot. If you like babes, see the Legh monument at Fulham, London, and go to Bishop's Tawton, Devon; a naked babe in its mother's arms can be seen at Norton-in-Hales, Salop.

About this time, figures were sometimes shown seated. The best-known example is Francis Bacon (as if asleep after a good dinner) at St Michael's, St Albans. Equally remarkable is Lady Bacon at Culford, Suffolk. She is seated, and is surrounded by her family with one child on her lap; her first husband is lying under her feet and one does wonder if they had a sense of humour at that time! Two figures seated together as if carrying on a conversation can be seen at Lydiard Tregoze, Wilts, a church rich in monuments. At Churchill, Somerset, the wife is merely the shroud and the husband looks extremely surprised.

Wall monuments were very popular in this century and at the end of the preceding century. Figures are often shown kneeling at a prayer-desk (Hengrave, Suffolk), or as busts, a quaint monument being at Brent Knoll, Somerset. Divines seem to like this form, as at Steeple Langford and Bishopstone, near Salisbury, Wilts, and Orwell, Cambs. If only the head and shoulders are depicted, it is probably later in the period (Clavering, Essex).

Towards the end of the century, as at Withyham, Sussex (Sackville family), monuments begin to show the trend that was fully developed in the next century.

EIGHTEENTH-CENTURY
MONUMENTS

Black-and-white marble superseded alabaster at the end of the seventeenth century, and colour ceased. The stupendous monuments of this period will always be noticed because they often dominate and dwarf the church. The sculpture is as magnificent as reverence is lacking. Figures now often stand, and such a position does not produce humility, but rather self-glorification, which does, of course, coincide with the low state of the life of the Church. The attire was often classical costume and wigs.

Epitaphs at this time use the most pompous and verbose language to describe the innumerable merits of the deceased. If these were true, it must have been an ideal time in which to live!

Ostentatious monuments of standing figures can be seen to perfection at Bletchingley, Surrey (Clayton family) (the same son can be seen again by himself at Ickenham, Middx), Shute, Devon (Pole family), Boxted, Suffolk (Pl. 39) (Poley family), Yarnton, Oxon (Spencer family), and Wanstead, Essex (Josiah Child).

Huge monuments with varying attitudes can also be well studied at Warkton, Northants (Montagu family), Redgrave, Suffolk (Lord Chief Justice Holt), and Steeple Bumpstead, Essex (Bendyshe family). At Strensham, Worcs, Sir Francis Russell reclines whilst his wife weeps over him and points upwards in the direction in which she hopes he has gone!

Four churches with delightful monuments to children alone must be specially mentioned: Elford,

Staffs, Great Barrington, Glos, Ashbourne, Derbyshire, and Chilham, Kent (also the famous one at Lichfield Cathedral, by Chantrey). From Tudor times onwards, the names of the sculptors are frequently known. From among so many, mention should be made of Maximilian Colt, Nicholas Stone, the Stantons, Epiphanius Evesham, Scheemakers, Rysbrack, Roubiliac, Nollekens, Flaxman and Chantrey.

CARTOUCHE TABLETS

These are a type of wall monument common in the seventeenth and eighteenth centuries. They are usually of marble and are like a sheet of paper with the sides curled up; the inscription is in the centre and above may be a coat of Arms and crest (p. 117).

LEDGER STONES

These massive floor slabs of seventeenth or early eighteenth century date are usually made from a bluish-grey stone. The armorial carving at the head of the slab and the inscription below are normally works of art, but all the average visitor does is to tread upon them. Holy Trinity, Hull, has many.

BRASSES

More brasses remain in England than in the whole of Europe, and they are most common in Kent, Essex, East Anglia and Oxon; then in the other Home Counties. The metal (latten) was manufactured before the Reformation exclusively in Flanders and Germany. The engraving, however, is English, for Continental brasses were on rectangular plates with the whole surface engraved. The English artist cut out his figures and bedded them into a slab of Purbeck marble or stone; but he often engraved elaborate canopies similar to those above carved effigies.

There are a few Flemish brasses in England, the finest being at St Margaret's, King's Lynn (two), St Albans Cathedral, Newark, Notts, and Wensley, North Riding.

The oldest brass figure is to Sir John Daubernoun, at Stoke D'Abernon, Surrey (1277), followed by Sir Roger de Trumpington at Trumpington, Cambs (1289). The finest brass of a knight is, however, Sir Robert de Bures at Acton, Suffolk (1302). He and Sir Robert de Setvans at Chartham, Kent (1306), have the crossed legs favoured at this time with carved figures. The earliest lady is Margaret de Camoys, Trotton, Sussex (about 1310).

All the brasses of this early period are as excellent as anything produced later. The figures are nearly life-size, and the engraving is more deeply cut than subsequently. Chain armour was then worn, to be replaced by plate armour.

In the fifteenth century small figures of children appear beneath their parents (five daughters and thirteen sons being on a brass at Brightwell Baldwin, Oxon); shroud brasses are introduced, the deceased being shown in a sheet (Digswell, Herts, and Aylsham, Norfolk), and mural brasses are occasionally used. By the end of that century figures tend to become stiff, the shading is overdone, and decline begins.

Heraldry on armour and on ladies' mantles was always popular, colour being used.

Special types are floriated crosses (particularly for ecclesiastics and civilians) (Hildersham, Cambs) and bracket brasses (Upper Hardres, Kent). Brasses of hearts, alone or in conjunction with figures, may also be found (Fawsley, Northants).

The armour of a knight will, of course, be an infallible clue as to date, as also the dress and head-dress of ladies. The last includes types known as reticulated, crespine, horned, mitred, butterfly, pedimental or kennel, and, after the Reformation, the Paris or Mary head-dress. Civilians are depicted at all times, and dating is as easy by the hair and beard as by the costume.

Clergy are usually shown in Mass vestments (Higham Ferrers, Northants), or in a cope, and sometimes the latter has saints on its orphreys (as at Bottesford, Leics, and Castle Ashby, Northants). As vestments did not alter, dating is difficult, but hair can give an indication; it was curly in the earlier medieval period and then at a later date hung straight down. Occasionally a priest was commemorated just by a chalice—particularly in Norfolk (Bawburgh). An archbishop wearing full vestments is splendidly shown in the brass to Thomas Cranley, Archbishop of Dublin, 1417, in the chapel of New College, Oxford.

Not many monastic brasses remain. Thomas Neolond, Prior of Lewes, 1433, at Cowfold, Sussex, is, however, one of the finest brasses anywhere, with a most elaborate canopy with figures. There is an abbess at Elstow, Beds. The dress of an abbess or nun is very similar to that of a widow (Draycot Cerne, Wilts).

Those connected with universities often appear in academical dress. (The majority, of course, are in and around Oxford and Cambridge, but Surlingham, Norfolk, has a good example.) Judges are also shown in their robes (Deerhurst, Glos, and see p. 203).

Post-Reformation brasses continue to depict the changing fashions. Brasses became popular again in Elizabeth's reign. Of the seventeenth century two are of special note: Sir Edward Filmer and family, 1629, at East Sutton, Kent, and Samuel Harsnett, Archbishop of York, 1631, at Chigwell, Essex.

In some medieval brasses husband and wife are hand in hand as in some carved effigies. Examples are at Chrishall, Essex, Draycot Cerne, Wilts, South Acre, Norfolk, and Trotton, Sussex.

Scenes of the Annunciation and the Resurrection can sometimes be found above the figures, but most common is a representation of the Holy Trinity, as at Childrey, Berks, and Hildersham, Cambs.

Inscriptions on brasses are always of interest, and sometimes they exist without any effigy. Their lettering, language and genealogy should be carefully studied.

Lettering and language can be a useful clue to date. Until the mid fourteenth century, Lombardic characters were employed, then black-letter until the seventeenth century, when Roman lettering was introduced. In the fourteenth century Norman-

French was often used, Latin in the fifteenth century, and English in the sixteenth century. Inscriptions to ecclesiastics, however, are almost invariably in Latin at all periods.

That a brass engraving was as respected as a figure carved in any material is proved by the fact that one of the finest monuments in the whole country—the Percy tomb in Beverley Minster, East Riding (Pl. 40)—had a brass and not a carved figure.

Palimpsest brasses are not uncommon. They are brasses that have been used twice. This could occur by substituting a new inscription on an earlier figure or by altering the figures themselves, but the most usual method is by engraving the back of an earlier brass. The latter would have been plunder from an English or Dutch church at the Reformation or earlier, or just shop-waste. It is useful to hang up such a brass on hinges so that both of its sides can be seen. For example, an inscription or figure of say 1540 may be on the back of a plate with part of a figure of a knight of say 1340 on its original front. An interesting study is therefore to try to find out in what churches the remainder of the 1340 knight can now be found. To give one instance, a brass at Yealmpton, Devon, is palimpsest, and another part of its original figure can be seen at Denham, near Eye, Suffolk—rather far apart.

Brasses may be found in the most unlikely places. They are often under mats, for protection. The best part of the church may, therefore, be under a mat, so always pick up anything you can in an old church (within reason, of course, and replace it). Numerous churchs have indents—stone slabs showing the outline of former brasses which have been picked up and not replaced—probably during the Cromwellian period.

Centres of the medieval woollen trade are often rich in brasses, as at Northleach and Cirencester, Glos, and All Saints', Stamford, Lincs. Tattershall, Lincs, is also notable.

The sanctuary floor covered with fine brasses can be seen at Digswell, Herts, where the old church has been effectively enlarged by adding a new church at the side. The most splendid display, however, not only in this country, but in the whole world, is at Cobham, Kent. There are no less than nineteen magnificent brasses, many with fine canopies, to members of the great Cobham family and the clergy who staffed the collegiate church.

Lastly, a word on brass-rubbing. It is a most satisfying and rewarding hobby. With a roll of detail paper, black heel-ball, and the incumbent's permission, one obtains a wonderful impression of the brass on the paper. One may have to crouch in an awkward position and one's hand may soon become tired, but, as with everything else in life, the more one puts into it, the more one gets out of it. The harder one rubs, the finer the result. Determination and perseverance will bring a reward that will last a lifetime. You will indeed be able to see the brass better on your paper than by looking at the original. The rubbings can then be cut out, mounted on linen, and hung on a wall.

The illustrations (pages 198–206) are a complete record from the thirteenth century to the seventeenth century of every type of armour, civil costume and ladies' dresses and head-dresses. In addition, of course, one's wardrobe of rubbings must contain the different types of ecclesiastical vestments, monks' and nuns' habits and academical and judicial costume.

STAINED GLASS

The earliest stained glass (more correctly termed painted glass) is of the twelfth century, and the finest remaining is at Canterbury Cathedral. Dorchester Abbey, Oxon, has four remarkable little windows completely filled with glass of that period, and there is another at Brabourne, Kent. Early figures are often in attitudes familiar in Byzantine art.

For thirteenth-century glass Canterbury Cathedral again is famous, and some fine glass of this period can also be seen at Aldermaston, Berks; Pl. 4 of the Annunciation gives an idea of the gorgeous colours, deep red and blue predominating. In this century grisaille glass was introduced, which was white glass with foliage patterns so arranged that the leadwork made patterns; sometimes it was relieved with lines of colour.

In the fourteenth century, picture panels on the grisaille glass became popular, as at Merton College, Oxford; other examples are at Selling, Kent, Chetwode, Bucks, and Stanton Harcourt, Oxon.

Previously each colour had to be leaded separately, but in the fourteenth century yellow stain was discovered, which meant that it could be painted on

Plate 37

1. Lydiard Tregoze, Wilts, Royal Arms.

2. Hoveton St Peter, Norfolk, hatchment.

3. Ripple, Worcs, misericord depicting reaping in August.

4. Dorchester Abbey, Oxon, medieval effigy of a knight.

Plate 38

1. Ashwellthorpe, Norfolk.
2. Strelley, Notts. Pre-Reformation monuments.
3. Wellington, Somerset, 17th-century monument with 28 figures.
4. Chillingham, Northumberland, monument of 1443, with saints and angels.

Plate 39 1. Elmley Castle, Worcs, 17th-century monument. 2. Slindon, Sussex, 16th-century wooden effigy. 3. Swinbrook, Oxon, Tudor monument of lolling figures. 4. Boxted, Suffolk, 18th-century monuments.

Plate 40 1. Paignton, Devon, chantry chapel. 2. Beverley Minster, East Riding, Percy monument. 3. Deerhurst, Glos. 4. Eaton Bishop, Herefords. Two examples of 14th-century stained glass.

Plate 41

1. Besthorpe, Norfolk, piscina and sedilia combined.
2. Hawton, Notts, Easter sepulchre.
3. Swinbrook, Oxon, altar rails.
4. Croft, North Riding, elevated 18th-century family pew.

Plate 42

1. Carleton Rode, Norfolk, Elizabethan Communion table.

2. Walpole St Peter, Norfolk, Perpendicular chancel.

3. Drayton, Berks, alabaster reredos.

4. Thornham Parva, Suffolk, 14th-century wooden reredos with panels of the Crucifixion and saints.

Plate 43 1. Ashburton, Devon, brass candelabrum. 2. Cirencester, Glos, 15th-century cope. 3. Hamstall Ridware, Staffs, medieval chalice and paten. Note the Manus Dei on the latter. 4. Watton, Norfolk, wooden beggar alms box.

Plate 44 1. Denston, Suffolk, a typical East Anglian church.
2. Puxton, Somerset, very quaint. 3. Altarnun, Cornwall, typically
Cornish. 4. Amberley, Sussex, Norman and Early English.

white or coloured glass for features, crowns and the like. A lesser discovery was abrasion whereby coated ruby glass could be scraped to show the white glass below; formerly, for example, each of the three golden lions of England had to be leaded into its ruby field, whereas now the glass could be abraded in the shape of lions and stained yellow. In the early sixteenth century brown enamel paint might be applied. Apart from these exceptions, however, throughout the medieval period each colour was a separate piece of glass surrounded by its leadwork.

In the fourteenth century, canopies were becoming taller, heraldy was introduced (Froyle, Hants, and Wimpole, Cambs), borders contained a variety of designs, and figures usually show the well-known "s" curve or bend instead of being entirely erect; this gives a life-like appearance and invariably indicates the date. All colours can now be found, but particularly red, green, yellow and brown, and they are of a very rich deep tone which has never been excelled. Good examples can be seen at York Minster, Oxford Cathedral in the Latin Chapel, Tewkesbury Abbey, Stanford, Northants, Checkley, Staffs, Eaton Bishop, Herefords (Our Lady and Child, Pl. 40, are lovely), and Deerhurst, Glos (Pl. 40). The lettering of inscriptions, as with brasses, can also, of course, be a useful clue to date.

In the fifteenth century, the Perpendicular window tracery gave every possible scope to the glass painter, whose art was then reaching its highest point of development. He could insert his figures of saints in the rectangular panels, which was quite impossible with the earlier Flowing tracery. Large

Perpendicular east windows with their original glass can be seen at Gloucester Cathedral (the largest window in England), St Peter Mancroft, Norwich, East Harling, Norfolk, and Langport, Somerset. There is splendid fifteenth-century glass throughout Great Malvern Priory, Worcs. In the West Riding the visitor to Thornhill and Almondbury will be well rewarded.

At this time the colours were generally lighter with much red, white and blue, and much yellow stain on white glass.

Canopies now become still taller and heraldry becomes more popular, and frequently the donors of the glass are depicted in the lower panels, as can be seen at Long Melford, Suffolk, and South Mimms, Middx.

Scenes from the Old Testament are rare, but exist at Great Malvern Priory, Worcs, and St Neot, Cornwall. Events in Our Lord's life are almost entirely confined to His infancy and Passion; the reason is that men's minds were set upon Redemption which was begun by His birth and achieved by His death (noticed in connection with wall-paintings. A typical crucifixion group with St Mary and St John, and donors below, is at Winscombe, Somerset.

Type and anti-type were popular, the idea being that Old Testament tincidents foretold those of the New Testament. Sometimes apostles hold a scroll with a part of the Creed (Drayton Beauchamp, Bucks and Nettlestead, Kent), and they may be paired with prophets (Isaiah, Jeremiah, and others), as at Fairford, Glos. Prophets never have haloes or emblems.

St Margaret (Combs, Suffolk) and St Catherine (Deerhurst, Glos) (Pl. 40) were always favourites amongst the saints. A most popular subject for glass was the Tree of Jesse. From the figure of Jesse rises a thick stem branching out to form frames for kings and prophets culminating in figures of the Blessed Virgin Mary and Child. An example can be seen at St Mary's, Shrewsbury, and there is a unique one combined with the stonework of the window at Dorchester Abbey, Oxon (both these windows being of the fourteenth century). Margaretting, Essex, and Leverington, Cambs, have examples of the fifteenth century.

Windows showing the Seven Sacraments (p. 105) and the Seven Works of Mercy (p. 113) were also popular, the former being represented at Crudwell, Wilts, and Doddiscombsleigh, Devon, and the latter at All Saints', North Street, York. It was usual to show the Seven Sacraments grouped around a central figure of Christ from Whose Wounds streams of blood flow into each sacrament.

The Nine Orders of Angels constantly appear, especially in East Anglia. The Nine Orders are Seraphim, Cherubim, Thrones, Dominions, Virtues, Powers, Principalities, Archangels and Angels, and the number of wings may be six, four or two. Figures of angels may often be found, particularly in tracery lights at the tops of windows, when the glass of the saints has long since been destroyed; they may hold musical instruments, censers, scrolls or shields. Sometimes they are in albs and sometimes they are feathered (Yarnton, Oxon). The latter type often wear white scarves, have hands in adoration, and are shown on a wheel to indicate speed and eternity.

The influence of the Renaissance can be well seen in two magnificent examples: the chapel of King's College, Cambridge, and Fairford church, Glos. This church has every window filled with lovely glass, almost all original, the church and its glass being due to the generosity of a rich wool merchant and his son. Hillesden, Bucks, has such glass.

The art of the glass painter in the early seventeenth century can be studied in the chapels of several Oxford colleges (Lincoln, Wadham and University); enamels were now mostly used instead of the medieval pot-metals, leaded outlines disappeared, and small leaded rectangular panes took their place.

Anyone interested in old glass will, however, make York his centre for a long holiday. The Minster itself is unrivalled in this country, and then there are the numerous parish churches in the City of York, nearly all of which have much of their original glass. There is, for example, Holy Trinity, Goodramgate, with a splendid east window; a number of saints depict family life, and a curious detail is that in two representations of the Holy Trinity the Son is not shown on the Cross. Very special mention must, however, be made of All Saints', North Street. Amongst many saints is St Christopher, and there is a charming light showing St Anne teaching her child, St Mary, to read. In addition to the Works of Mercy, there is a most remarkable window showing the last fifteen days of the world. It would seem that the scenes are not far removed from the result of an atomic explosion (but the Church stands for something that will never end).

There were, of course, different centres of painting throughout the country and each had its own local characteristics.

In studying medieval windows it must always be remembered that the glass painter showed scenes in a homely fashion as they would be known to him in this country; for example, the Last Supper might often be shown as in any English cottage, and the Entry into Jerusalem as in any village street. A fire may be shown in a Nativity scene, indicating that the artist could visualize Christmas only in connection with our cold climate.

If stained glass appears silvery when seen from outside it is most probably ancient.

The real beauty of medieval glass cannot be conveyed by words or black-and-white illustrations. In their prime the windows would have been like the richest jewels sparkling with gorgeous colours. One must study carefully what remains and then one will never drop the brick that the gaudy Victorian east window is the best part of the church! Some glass of that period, however, is better than others, and some excellent work is being done today.

We have mentioned churches that have much notable old glass in the hope that some may be visited; but the majority of old churches have fragments somewhere, and to detect them will now be the aim of the visitor.

A subject cannot be treated in stained glass as it can in wall-paintings. It is not a picture. Each light must be complete in itself, usually with one or two large figures making the subject quite clear (not always followed today).

Modern glass depicting the church itself and the countryside around it is, however, attractive when seen at close quarters. We can mention such at Nettlecombe, Somerset, Colne Engaine, Essex, Ringstead, Norfolk, Dean Prior, Devon, and Pinner, Middx. At Selborne, Hants, is a window of St Francis with every bird mentioned in Gilbert White's book.

Bright colours often predominate in present-day glass. The symbols of the Four Evangelists are shown amidst such brightness in two remarkable windows at Wellingborough, Northants.

SQUINTS

These are apertures, usually oblique, cut through a wall, giving a view of an altar. If one prefers a long Greek term, hagioscope can be used. Squints are very common and are of all periods. They vary in size and design, but are usually rectangular and quite plain. There is an exceptionally long one at West Chiltington, Sussex.

They may be directed to a side altar, but more usually to the High Altar, and very often they are on one or both sides of a chancel arch; but they may occur almost anywhere. It must be remembered that a squint may sometimes be directed to the original site of the High Altar before it was moved eastward on the subsequent lengthening of the chancel.

In Cornwall and Pembrokeshire some very large squints actually form a passage-way.

The squint may have had several different uses. Some were obviously used in connection with ringing the Sanctus bell so that the bell-ringer could see the altar (Loxton, Somerset), but there is no doubt that the majority were intended for the congregation to view the Elevation of the Host.

LOW-SIDE WINDOWS

These are sometimes called "leper windows", but lepers were not, of course, allowed in public, and their hospitals had their own chapels. There has been more controversy as to the use of these windows than about anything else connected with an old church. It is sometimes stated that they were used for confessions, but from their position this would mean that the penitent might have to lie on his stomach or climb to the top of a ladder! The better opinion appears to be that a small bell was rung from them at the Sanctus and at the Consecration of the Elements, so that the Real Presence might be known outside.

These windows are most often found at the west end of the chancel on the south side, but sometimes on the north side (particularly if the village is on that side), or even on both sides. See p. 66.

The lower part of these windows was often separated from the upper part, no doubt for a wooden shutter, as still remains at Melton Constable, Norfolk. Moreover, this example has a stone seat and a stone desk for a book for the server or parish clerk, who could follow the service and ring the bell at the appropriate moment. In many churches, however, the Sanctus bell was in its own turret at the east end of the nave (Eltisley, Cambs

Low-side window.
Melton Constable,
Norfolk.

Squint.
Irthlingborough,
Northants.

(Pl. 16), and Idbury, Oxon, with its original bell).

At Scarning and Salhouse, Norfolk, the original small bell rung inside, the sacring bell, still remains and is attached to the rood-screen.

In the latest churches today a server merely has to press a button in the sanctuary floor in front of him to ring a bell in the tower!

PISCINAS

A piscina is a drain in a niche in the wall, usually surmounted by an arch and ornamented, if at all, in the same manner as doorways and arches of its period. It is usually on the south side of the chancel near the High Altar. There may be two in the same wall, which, of course, indicates that the chancel has

Piscinas.
Carleton Rode, Norfolk.   Great Snoring, Norfolk.

been lengthened (the western one being the earlier of the two). They are also found at the east end of aisles and sometimes in other places and their presence always proves that there was an altar near by. Occasionally the drain is contained in a bracket projecting from the wall (Skelton, near York, North Riding, and Skipwith, East Riding), or the bracket takes the form of a capital on a small pillar (Finch-ampstead, Berks). These two types are usually of early date.

Sometimes the piscina is a double one having two drains, and this type can broadly be assigned to the reign of Edward I (1272-1307). There was then a separate drain for the lavabo (washing of the priest's fingers before the Consecration) and the ablutions or rinsing of the chalice. Before that period one drain was used for both, and since that date the ablutions have always been consumed by the priest.

There is a beautiful double piscina at Cherry Hinton, near Cambridge. The dog-tooth ornament confirms its date. A particularly elaborate double piscina for a small church is at Barnston, Essex, and there is another at Carleton Rode, Norfolk.

A local use in East Anglia is an angle piscina—cut out of the eastern jamb of a south window, with openings to the north and west, and often a shaft between them (Great Snoring, Norfolk).

At the back of the niche may be a shelf for the cruets of wine and water, and the lavabo bowl; today a credence table is usual.

In the finest examples the piscina is united with the sedilia in one design (see opposite).

There is often one feature in an old church which is unknown anywhere else. As an example, the piscina at Oare, Somerset, takes the form of a stone head held up by two hands. This remote church has hundreds of visitors owing to its connection with Lorna Doone. Near by is Culbone in a perfect setting with the smallest complete medieval church.

SEDILIA

These are seats, nearly always of stone. They are invariably found to the south of the altar and were used by the celebrant and his two assistants, the deacon and sub-deacon. They were occupied during the Creed and Gloria when the service was sung.

The number of seats is therefore usually three, but this number can vary. They are either graded towards the east or on the same level. In the English Use the celebrant sits to the east of the deacon and

12ᵗʰ. Cent.ʸ   13ᵗʰ. Cent.ʸ   14ᵗʰ. Cent.ʸ   15ᵗʰ. Cent.ʸ

String-courses.
(and abacus of capitals)

sub-deacon and not between them as in the modern Western Use. Very often the piscina and sedilia were constructed at the same time and are therefore of the same design, as at St Mary-de-Castro, Leicester (Norman); Monyash, Derbyshire (Transitional Norman); Cherry Hinton, Cambs (Early English); Hawton and Car Colston, Notts, Heckington, Lincs, Swavesey, Cambs, Besthorpe, Norfolk (Pl. 41), Sandiacre, Derbyshire, and Dorchester Abbey, Oxon (with small windows containing twelfth-century glass) (Decorated); and Adderbury, Oxon, (Perpendicular).

The simplest possible type is, of course, obtained

by lowering the sill of a window; usually, however, the canopies are most elaborate.

Wooden sedilia occur at Beverley Minster, East Riding, and Rodmersham, Kent.

Above the piscina and sedilia, but under the windows, may be a stone band which continues round the walls. This is called a "string-course", and its mouldings can be a useful clue in fixing the date of a wall.

PRIESTS' DOORS

In a side wall of the chancel is often a doorway that is much smaller than the main doorways. As its name suggests, it would be used by the priest for direct access to the chancel. It is more often on the south side than on the north side.

EASTER SEPULCHRES

An Easter Sepulchre is always situated on the north side of the chancel, usually in the sanctuary. The Blessed Sacrament was placed in an aperture of this structure on Good Friday and remained there until early on Easter Day. Most churches must have used a temporary structure or the top of an altar tomb. A few special structures of stone, mostly of the fourteenth century, do, however, remain. Hawton, Notts (Pl. 41), is the most elaborate, and there are others at Heckington and Navenby, Lincs, Patrington, East Riding, and Northwold, Norfolk. The carving usually shows the Resurrection with the sleeping soldiers, and, above, a representation of the Ascension.

AUMBRIES

Near an altar, and often on the north side, a plain
oblong opening sometimes remains. It originally had
a door, which still exists at Great Walsingham, Norfolk, and Rothersthorpe, Northants. The altar plate
would have been kept there, and other valuables
were stored in the chest; aumbry and chest therefore represent the modern vestry, for medieval
sacristies are not common. There is a Norman one
at Hemel Hempstead, Herts.

Today in the Church of England the Blessed
Sacrament is more usually reserved in an aumbry in
a wall or in a tabernacle on an altar rather than in
a pyx (see p. 166).

ALTAR RAILS

These were gradually introduced after the Reformation to protect the altar when screens were disappearing, and they became popular in the time of
Archbishop Laud in the seventeenth century to
prevent the altar being moved into the body of the
church (as desired by the Puritans) and to prevent
dogs getting in. They are therefore nearly always
early seventeenth century and of wood; they
usually extend from wall to wall, but sometimes
they enclose the altar on three sides (Elmsett,
Suffolk) or occasionally on four sides (Lyddington,
Rutland).

The balusters often have a central bulge (Cliffe-
at-Hoo, Kent, and Swinbrook, Oxon, Pl. 41), or
they may take the form of columns (Great Walsingham, Norfolk). The twisted baluster type (Great

Staughton, Hunts, and Branscombe, Devon) is probably of the second half of the seventeenth century.

HIGH ALTAR

This is the focal point of the whole church. Before the Reformation altars were of stone and the tops or mensa sometimes remain, although not often in their original position. They can always be identified by five crosses indented on them, one at each corner and one in the centre.

After the Reformation, however, altars were made of wood, and Communion tables of Elizabethan and Jacobean date are handsomely carved and have bulbous legs (Carleton Rode, Norfolk, Pl. 42, Blyford, Suffolk, and Minehead, Somerset).

Before the Reformation the number of candles on the altar was probably two, as can be seen on the Seven Sacrament font at Gresham, Norfolk. The cross, so familiar today, may then possibly have been the head of the processional cross placed upon the altar for the service. Today it is quite usual, and most effective, to have six candles and crucifix. It is not correct to place anything else, such as flowers, on the altar itself.

The altar should be long and low and covered with three linen cloths. There is usually a frontal, the colour changing according to the season of the Church's year as mentioned on p. 187.

The High Altar is the central point of the church, because there heaven and earth meet in the service commanded by Our Lord, "Do this in remembrance of Me". Angels and men join in the worship of the Holy Trinity, pleading before the eternal Father the timeless sacrifice of Christ, once offered on Calvary. The service of the Holy Communion, Eucharist, or Mass is His perpetual memorial and the chief purpose for which the church was built.

REREDOSES

Our medieval churches must have had several reredoses as there were then several altars in each church. The reredos formed a back to the altar. They were of stone, alabaster, or painted wooden panels, or perhaps paintings on the wall, as at St Albans Cathedral. A fine one of alabaster is at Drayton, Berks (Pl. 42, showing the Entombment). There are others at Elham, Kent, and Yarnton, Oxon.

Ones of stone with figures of Christ and the Apostles in niches can be seen at Bampton and Somerton, Oxon, the latter appropriately representing the Last Supper. Niches sometimes still remain but without their figures.

The wonderful stone altar screens or retables in Winchester and St Albans cathedrals and in the chapels of New College, All Souls' College and Magdalen College, Oxford, are well known. Similar ones in parish churches exist at Christchurch Priory, Hants (Pl. 24), and Ottery St Mary, Devon. There is a fine modern reredos in colour at Wymondham Abbey, Norfolk.

There is a most remarkable fourteenth-century wooden reredos at the charming small thatched

church of Thornham Parva, Suffolk (Pl. 42); it has
painted panels of the Crucifixion with St Mary and
St John and other saints. Splendid painted wooden
panels of a reredos also remain at Norwich Cathedral and Romsey Abbey, Hants.

On the screen at Attleborough, Norfolk (Pl. 36),
are three tall painted panels on each side of its
doorway, which were reredoses for the nave altars.
The screen at Ranworth, also in that county, serves
the same purpose.

Victorian reredoses by contrast are often ugly, of
massive white marble, and they usually spoil the
east end. The English village church really requires
nothing more than just its east window, and no
part of it should ever be blocked. An effective
arrangement is to have a dossal curtain as a background, or to surround the altar on three sides by
some bright textile (preferably crimson and gold)
with two or four riddel posts which might support
figures of angels holding candles.

ALTAR CANOPIES

Dignity is achieved by a canopy. Above an altar, the
roof may be more richly decorated, or a tester may
be suspended, as at Clun, Salop.

PYX

The general English practice was to reserve the
Blessed Sacrament in a pyx covered with some costly
fabric and suspended in front of the High Altar.
Only one original pyx cloth is in existence, from

Hessett, Suffolk (in the British Museum). A pyx pulley socket remains at West Grinstead, Sussex.

LENT VEILS

The sanctuary was veiled from sight during the greater part of Lent. Hooks from which the veil was hung may still exist, as at Shillington, Beds, and Alfriston, Sussex. The rood and other figures were also then covered. (See also p. 178.)

EAST WINDOW

This will not, necessarily, be the largest window in the church, as so much will depend upon its date. It is, however, the one object in a church which everyone sees—and the one object which ought not to be seen at all if, as is unfortunately often the case, the glass is bad. If the glass is medieval, then we have beauty as originally intended.

Three lancets of early thirteenth-century date make a charming east end. For simple dignity they are unsurpassed and there are many such east ends in Sussex (see p. 58). A large Perpendicular east window, however, is uplifting with its vertical lines (see pp. 64 and 152).

On either side of the window may be large niches with elaborate canopies for figures of saints. The niche on the north side is usually occupied by a figure of the patron saint.

SANCTUARY CHAIRS

The place of honour in the stalls is the northern return stall on the south side (see p. 129). The place

of honour in the sanctuary is on the north side—
where the bishop sits when visiting the church. An
old chair or chairs, frequently Jacobean, may therefore often be found within the altar rails. A most
elaborate one with carvings of the Entry into Jerusalem and the Wise Men is at Ledbury, Herefords.
The stone sanctuary chair at Beverley Minster is
Saxon.

FLOWERS

It is, of course, appropriate that flowers—the beauty
of God in nature—should be prominent in a church
(except in Lent), more particularly at great festivals
and the Harvest Festival. One large bowl of flowers
on the north side of the chancel is now often seen
and is most effective. Flower Festivals are popular.

PRE-REFORMATION CHURCH PLATE

Ecclesiastical plate consisted of the Sacramental
plate, namely chalice and paten, together with cruets
for wine and water, pyx (for reservation of the
Sacred Host), ciborium (for its administration),
monstrance (for its exposition), censer (for incense),
pax (for the kiss of peace), chrismatory (for the holy
oils), and altar and processional crosses and candlesticks (p. 178). Inventories show how rich cathedrals
and churches were in the number and costliness of
their sacred vessels and plate. Very little survived
the Reformation, so that we now have only about
fifty-five chalices and ninety-five patens of pre-
Reformation date.

Chalices were then usually of silver-gilt, from six to eight inches in height, and consisted of a spreading base, a stem with a swelling or knob for handling easily, and a bowl.

The earliest chalices had a hemispherical bowl, short stem, and circular base, but from about 1350 to 1510 the bowl was conical or sugar-loaf shape, the knob was large and elaborate, sometimes with angels' heads or flowers, and the foot was hexagonal (to prevent rolling when laid on its side). The crucifixion was usually engraved on one side of the base.

Chalices of the Tudor period until the Reformation have a more shallow bowl and are more hemispherical again, the stem and knob are elaborate with architectural ornament, and the foot is a sixfoil or a wavy base. There is often an inscription on the bowl and sometimes on the base as well.

Chalices with their patens still remain at Hamstall Ridware, Staffs (Pl. 43), Beswick, East Riding, and Leominster Priory and Bacton, Herefords. Chalices without their patens can be found at Little Faringdon, Oxon, Combe Keynes, Dorset, and Wylye, Wilts.

The paten is a small, flat, circular cover for the chalice, but when in use, the Sacred Host is placed upon it. There is always a depression in the centre of the paten with a design. The Lamb of God is the earliest device, but later the Manus Dei, or hand of God in blessing, became common. These early patens had a depression that was circular or a quatrefoil (four hollows between cusps). Later in the fourteenth century and onwards the depression was a sixfoil. In the fifteenth and early sixteenth centuries the most usual design was the Vernicle or head of Christ, but in the latter period the device may be the sacred monogram IHS (p. 190), and the inscription round the rim, occasional before, is now habitual.

Rather curiously, nearly half of the pre-Reformation patens which remain are in Norfolk.

The earliest is of about 1220 at Weeke, Hants, with the design of the Lamb of God. An example of the Manus Dei is at Hamstall Ridware, Staffs (Pl. 43), and examples of the Vernicle can be found at Beeston Regis, Norfolk, Leominster Priory and Bacton, Herefords, and St Edmund's, Salisbury. The sacred monogram occurs at Buckhorn Weston, Dorset, Beswick, East Riding, and Walmer, Kent. A fine paten remains at Cliffe-at-Hoo, Kent, with an engraving of the Holy Trinity.

Occasionally a leather chalice case remains (Cawston, Norfolk).

New College, Oxford, possesses a medieval pax, and of censers and incense-boats the finest must be those from Ramsey Abbey, Hunts, which were buried in the Fens and are now in the Victoria and Albert Museum. Of altar or processional crosses we can mention the splendid example at Lamport, Northants.

POST-REFORMATION CHURCH PLATE

The restoration of the communion in both kinds to the laity demanded a larger vessel. In medieval times the laity had been denied receiving the precious Blood. The Communion cups of the time of Edward VI are plain with bell-shaped bowls and a conical stem without a knob. Probably not very many were made as the pre-Reformation chalices continued to be used.

In Elizabeth's reign, however, new cups were substituted. The bowl was now elongated in the form of an inverted bell, the stem was trumpet- or baluster-shaped with a knob, and the base was circular and plain. The paten also changed, for it was very slightly domed and the sunk part was deepened, the brim narrowed, and a rim or edge

Elizabethan
chalice and paten.

Dole cupboard.
Milton Ernest, Beds.

attached to fit as a cover. A small stem was now added to the back of the paten, which, of course, served as a foot and a handle, and made it easier to hold. Ornament consisted of an engraved band of foliage round the body of the cup (Digswell, Herts), and on the top of the cover. Sometimes the name of the parish was engraved on the cup (Dersingham and Sall, Norfolk). In some of the later cups the knob disappeared. Innumerable Elizabethan examples exist in all parts of the country (most of all, however, in Somerset). In Jacobean times, cups are larger and plainer, the bowl is a truncated cone and the stem has a thin projecting collar. After the Restoration chalices had capacious bowls, thick stems, and plain feet.

Large flagons replaced the small medieval cruets, and from the seventeenth century onwards they are of tall tankard shape.

EMBROIDERY

We also have evidence of the immense wealth of embroidered vestments and hangings possessed by English churches at the time of the Reformation. English needlework was renowned, for it was the finest in the world and was known as Opus Anglicanum.

It is a tragedy that so little remains. Most are fragments made into altar frontals. A number of copes remain unaltered, probably because they were not Mass vestments; they are mostly in museums or private ownership. (After the Reformation anything connected with the Mass became unpopular.)

The materials used were always of the finest, velvet being specially favoured, and great quantities of metal thread, always of pure gold and silver, were employed.

For decoration, angels on wheels (as in glass) were very popular, and also the lion mask, double-headed eagle and leopard's head with protruding tongue. Scenes from the life of Our Lord and the saints were shown most realistically.

Copes were often adorned with orphreys with figures of saints under canopies and in some of the most costly the whole fabric would be cloth of gold.

The most famous cope remaining is the Syon cope which belonged to the nuns of Syon Abbey, Isleworth, Middlesex. It is late thirteenth century and all the splendid figures show the "S" bend which was then becoming fashionable. It is now in the Victoria and Albert Museum.

Some idea of the beauty of this medieval work can still, however, be gained from Durham and Carlisle cathedrals and from churches. The enthusiast should see the cope and pair of altar frontals at Chipping Campden, Glos, the chasubles at Barnstaple, Devon, and Hullavington, Wilts, the parts of copes at East Langdon, Kent, Buckland, Glos, Culmstock, Devon, Great Bircham and Lyng, Norfolk, Careby, Lincs, Othery, Somerset, and Forest Hill, Oxon, the altar frontals at Alveley, Salop, and Baunton, Glos, and the desk-hanging made up from orphreys at Sutton Benger, Wilts. Pl. 43 illustrates part of a fifteenth-century cope at Cirencester, Glos. An embroidered burse (or corporal case) (see p. 187) remains at Wymondham Abbey, Norfolk. Medieval palls or hearse cloths can be seen at Dunstable Priory, Beds, and St Peter's, Sudbury, Suffolk.

At this point a word might be useful on vestments, more particularly in studying brasses. They have now returned to use in many churches. Broadly speaking they are the ordinary dress of earliest times, and the Church, being conservative, has not thought it necessary to make any change.

A cope, worn over cassock and surplice, is the vestment used in processions. It is secured in front by an elaborate morse. It can be worn by a deacon and even by a layman. In brasses, an almuce is generally seen under the cope; this is a large cape turned down over the shoulders and lined with fur, two long pendants hanging down in front.

The principal vestment is the chasuble which can be worn only by a priest. Over the cassock one vests in the following order: amice (of linen, worn round the neck, and sometimes with an embroidered apparel); alb (long, white, flowing garment with sleeves, and sometimes with embroidered apparels on the wrists and between the feet); girdle (to pull up the alb at the waist); stole (a narrow strip of embroidery, worn by a deacon over the left shoulder and under the right arm, by a priest crossed in front of the body, and by a bishop uncrossed); maniple (a short stole worn over the left wrist—this was the napkin to wipe off perspiration); and finally the chasuble, which is passed over the head through a hole in the middle. Front and back are pointed or circular (p. 205).

At a High Mass the deacon and sub-deacon wear the dalmatic and tunicle respectively—similar to the chasuble, but they have straight edges, are slit up the sides, and have short wide sleeves.

A bishop in Mass vestments is shown wearing all those relating to a priest as well as the dalmatic and tunicle and those relating to his Order, namely sandals, gloves, ring and mitre; in addition he holds his pastoral staff (its head being in the form of a shepherd's crook). An archbishop can always be distinguished by the pall (a Y-shaped loop of wool) worn over the chasuble, and he usually holds a cross-staff instead of a pastoral staff. The brass of the archbishop at New College, Oxford (p. 205) and the monument to Archbishop Chicheley, Canterbury Cathedral, show the complete attire.

In Elizabethan times and in the seventeenth century, devotion to the Church continued, as is proved by embroidery still so lovingly worked. Such embroidery can be well studied at Hollingbourne, Kent, Bacton, Herefords, Mattingley and St Mary Bourne, Hants, and Weston Favell, Northants. All are altar frontals, the last appropriately showing the Last Supper.

Today ornamental work is sometimes effectively bestowed upon hassocks (kneelers).

ORGANS

Before the Reformation most churches would have had an organ and its position was on the roof-loft, hence the meaning of organ loft. The Puritans strongly objected to joy as well as beauty, which may account for there being no pre-Reformation case left in England, though there is one at Old Radnor in Wales. At Framlingham, Suffolk, is a beautiful old organ case which was originally set up in Pembroke College Chapel, Cambridge, in 1674. Others may be seen at Winchcombe and Wotton-under-Edge, Glos.

The churches of the City of London which were rebuilt by Sir Christopher Wren after the Great Fire of 1666 vied with one another over their organs, both in the tone of the instruments themselves and in the beauty of their cases. The names of Renatus Harris and Father Smith as organ builders are well known. Some organs were unfortunately lost in the last war, but many still remain, often without any restoration having been necessary. We must mention in particular the organs at St Clement's, Eastcheap, and St Magnus, London Bridge; on the latter was first introduced the swell or sliding shutter. Other fine examples are at St Stephen's, Walbrook, and St Sepulchre's, Holborn. To sit in a City church and listen to one of these fine instruments is indeed an uplifting experience.

For a splendid old organ case in a splendid old village church, one cannot do better than visit Stanford, Northants. The organ case at Great Yarmouth, Norfolk, is a good example of modern colour work.

Old barrel organs can be found at Wood Rising, Norfolk, Avington, Hants, Cardeston, Salop, Farnham, West Riding, and Wardley, Rutland.

WEST GALLERY AND MUSICAL INSTRUMENTS

After the destruction of rood-lofts at the Reformation, the village orchestra in the west gallery was a leading feature of church life until the middle of the last century when a surpliced choir of men and boys was placed in the chancel. At Strensham, Worcs, the panels of the rood-loft themselves have actually been transferred to form the front of the west gallery. Old prints often show such galleries in use with large and varied musical instruments being played. At the small remote church of Trentishoe, Devon, the west gallery retains the hole through which protruded the bow of the double-bass.

Some of the instruments of these orchestras survive, as for example a pitch-pipe at Moreton Morrell, Warwicks, and Ditchling, Sussex, a vamping horn (huge trumpet) at East Leake, Notts, and Braybrooke, Northants, a bassoon at Harringworth, Northants, and Good Easter, Essex, a clarinet at South Muskham, Notts, and a bass-fiddle at Giggleswick, West Riding.

Some galleries within west towers were erected in pre-Reformation times, as at Cawston and Worstead, Norfolk, but generally west galleries were erected after the Reformation to accommodate the musical performers. Good examples of such galleries of the early seventeenth century are at Moreton Say, Salop, Puddletown, Dorset, and East Brent, Somerset.

Side galleries to the north and south of the nave might have been added later if increased accommodation was necessary, thus blocking up the church. An example still remains at Whitby, North Riding.

LIGHTS OF A CHURCH

Cressets were cups hollowed in stone and filled with oil with a floating wick. Cresset stones with a number of such cups remain at Westow, East Riding (with a Saxon rood on the reverse), Collingham, West Riding, and Lewannick, Cornwall.

Even in medieval days a lamp burned in the sanctuary in honour of the Blessed Sacrament. Next in importance were the lights that burned before the rood. Candles were often placed on the rood-beam, and in addition there might have been a corona or circle of perhaps twenty candles suspended in front of the rood. Pulleys for this and the Lent veil (see p. 167) sometimes remain in the roof above (Ubbeston, Suffolk).

Candles were attached to the lectern in the middle of the choir, and altar candlesticks have been used since the thirteenth century. Four outstanding ones from early in that century are at St Thomas's, Bristol. The finest examples of all periods are, of course, in cathedrals, but the parish churches of Harthill, West Riding, and Buckland, Surrey, have good seventeenth-century pairs.

Two thirteenth-century iron brackets ornamented with cocks and with prickets (or spikes) for candles remain at Rowlstone, Herefords. One magnificent medieval bronze candelabrum exists. It belonged to the Temple Church, Bristol, and it is now in the Cathedral. It was the forerunner of the candelabra or chandeliers which were so popular in the seventeenth and eighteenth centuries. They are of brass, having usually two tiers of branched candlesticks on gracefully curved stems springing from a central globe, which generally bears the name of the donor and the date. They are found throughout the country and they always enhance a church. From so many, we can only give a few examples quite at random: Stogumber, Axbridge and Wedmore, Somerset, Ightham, Kent, Braunton and Ashburton (Pl. 43), Devon, Lingfield, Surrey, Mayfield, Sussex, and Bourne and Frampton, Lincs. Often the suspension rod is of fine wrought ironwork, as at Lingfield.

Red, White and Blue Lights

The Sacramental Presence can always be recognized by a white light burning near by.

A red light sometimes hangs above an altar, and a blue light is placed before a figure of the Virgin and her Divine Child. It is most appropriate to have such a figure, showing that God in His love took human form to redeem us and to show us what He is like and how we should live.

FAMILY PEWS

Such pews followed after chantry chapels (p. 138) had ceased. In some cases, as at Lavenham and Kedington, Suffolk, chantry enclosures became family pews. They could be open above, as in the splendid Elizabethan example at Holcombe Rogus, Devon, or, more usually, they had a canopy, making them rather like a four-poster bed, a good example being at Tawstock, Devon, with a miniature coloured roof. Others may be found at Tibenham, Norfolk, Stokesay, Salop, Rycote, Oxon, and Warbleton, Sussex. At Croft, North Riding (Pl. 41), is a remarkable elevated eighteenth-century family pew; it is reached by a wide balustraded staircase.

Later the pew developed into a cosy furnished apartment with comfortable upholstered armchairs, padded benches, table, carpet, fireplace, and a separate entrance direct from the big house. Gatton, Surrey, is a perfect example.

Fireplaces may also be seen at Heveningham, Suffolk, Colebrooke, Devon, and in the beautifully restored church of Cottesbrooke, Northants.

CHEST-CUPBOARDS AND DOLE CUPBOARDS

A chest-cupboard, almery or hutch has a door or doors in front. It is found only occasionally, a notable example being at Louth, Lincs, of about 1500.

A later form known as a dole cupboard, or shelf, was for bread for the poor bequeathed by some kind benefactor. Such a cupboard was pierced in front so that there could be a good current of air. Examples may be seen at St Albans Cathedral, All Saints', Hereford, and Milton Ernest, Beds (p. 171). Bequest Boards are quite common.

BANNER-STAVE LOCKERS

Processions were a feature of medieval church life and long staves were necessary to bear aloft banners and crucifixes. Provision for storing these was in a tall narrow recess up to twelve feet high in the wall. They are most common in east Suffolk and east Norfolk. The one at Barnby, Suffolk, still retains its original door.

SWORD-RESTS

The churches of the City of London have much good ironwork, but perhaps the most exquisite craftsmanship is bestowed on sword-rests. The designs are always intricate and there are a number of coloured coats of Arms.

Sword-rests are the stands for the sword and mace when the Lord Mayor attends in state. They can, of course, be found in other cities. In London there are splendid examples at St Mary Abchurch, near Cannon Street.

LIBRARIES AND CHAINED BOOKS

There are about fifty important libraries in parish churches. The largest library of chained books is at Hereford Cathedral with about 2,000 volumes, of which about 1,500 are chained. All Saints' Church in that city also has a notable library of 328 volumes cunningly chained.

Other large libraries with chained books are at Cartmel Priory, Lancs, Grantham, Lincs, and Wimborne Minster, Dorset. The seventeenth-century cupboards and fittings of the library at Langley Marish, Bucks, are unaltered and are charming.

Individual chained books on stands are often found. They would probably be the Bible, Erasmus's *Paraphrases*, Jewel's *Defence of the Apology*, or Foxe's *Book of Martyrs*. Examples are at Kingsthorpe, Northants, Wiggenhall St Mary the Virgin,

Norfolk, Sherborne St John, Hants, and Cumnor, Berks.

Chaining of individual books was not a post-Reformation introduction; many pre-Reformation books were chained. Founding of church libraries, of course, became more popular and necessary after the Reformation when libraries which had mostly been provided by monasteries were unfortunately disappearing.

We have noted that every part of an old church was beautiful and that it was gorgeous with colour, for nothing could be too good for the House of God. This certainly also applied to the books used in the services. Many missals, psalters, gospels, and other books have survived and are now usually in museums. The wonderful illuminations and the time and care given to the lettering prove the same inspiration and devotion as with the building and its accessories—a burning love for the Creator of all things.

TILES

Ordinary flooring of early small churches would probably have been nothing more than stamped earth, which was covered with rushes for warmth. Stone slabs or plain tiles might have been laid later. Decorated tiles were being made, but they would have been used sparingly in the average church—in chancels and chapels and around altars. In an important building the floor would be entirely composed of decorated encaustic tiles, as can be seen to this day in the Chapter House of Westminster Abbey.

There were usually two colours only, red and yellow. The subjects consisted mainly of architectural and geometrical figures, interspersed with human or grotesque heads, symbolical figures (particularly a fish, p. 190), and a great number of armorial bearings. The fleur-de-lys was very popular.

Consecration cross.
Carleton Rode, Norfolk.

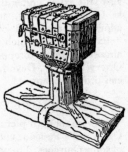

Alms box.
Loddon, Norfolk.

Examples of medieval tiles remain throughout the country, particularly in Worcestershire and Devon. More or less complete floors remain at Hailes, Glos, and West Hendred, Berks, and examples can be well studied at Watchet and Old Cleeve, Somerset, Cadeleigh, Westleigh and Haccombe, Devon, Launcells, Cornwall, Brook, Kent, and Great and Little Malvern Priories and Bredon, Worcs.

CONSECRATION CROSSES

At the consecration the bishop anointed twelve

places inside the church and twelve places on its outside. Those inside were usually marked by twelve crosses painted on the walls, and occasionally one or two still remain. Quite a number, however, can be seen at Edington, Wilts, Crosthwaite, Cumberland, Holnest, Dorset, and Carleton Rode, Norfolk. One also still exists under the remarkable wall-painting at Chaldon, Surrey, and two bright red crosses adorn the east wall of Bishop's Sutton, Hants.

Exterior ones, which were probably carved, have almost invariably disappeared, but Uffington, Berks, Ottery St Mary, Devon, and Moorlynch, Somerset, can provide examples.

STATIONS OF THE CROSS

These are modern pictures or carvings of scenes of Our Lord's Passion, and may be seen on the walls of some churches. They should be bright and colourful.

CHURCHWARDENS' STAVES

Churchwardens are the guardians of the parish church. In the nave their staves can often be seen and these may be surmounted by a crown and mitre respectively or by some emblem connected with the church, as, for example, cats at Whiston, Northants, the church having been built by the Catesby family in 1534.

ACOUSTIC JARS

These are further proof that the medieval churchman knew everything that was worth knowing about a church. He was not going to tolerate not hearing sufficiently, and he most effectively devised the first loudspeakers. Earthenware jars which have been found beneath choir stalls were undoubtedly placed there for improving the sound of the building. These vessels were also frequently embedded in chancel walls and occasionally in nave walls. Examples still remain at Lyddington, Rutland, Denford, Northants, and Tarrant Rushton, Dorset.

ALMS BOXES

A visit to an old church should be enjoyable. If so, it will be one's wish, not a burden, to place something in one of these boxes for the maintenance of the work of the Church and the upkeep of the fabric —simply out of gratitude for our heritage and that it may continue to function for hundreds of years to come as it has done for hundreds of years past.

The best pre-Reformation alms box is at Blythburgh, Suffolk. It is tall with three traceried panels in front. Pre-Reformation boxes also remain at Cawston and Loddon, Norfolk. If one is interested in ingenuity, one cannot do better than study the intricacies involved in making the contents of these last two boxes absolutely safe.

After the dissolution of the monasteries, the relief of the poor became a pressing necessity. Dated Elizabethan alms boxes remain at Hargrave, Northants, and Dovercourt, Essex. Seventeenth-century boxes are fairly numerous, and they often bear the words "Remember the Poor". Giggleswick, West Riding, and Manton, Rutland, have dated examples.

At Watton, Norfolk (Pl. 43), the box is held by a wooden figure of a beggar, dated 1639, and at Pinhoe, Devon, a particularly well-dressed gentleman calls himself "Ye Poor Man of Pinhoe, 1700". At St Teath, Cornwall, the Jacobean box is painted with figures. At Tunworth, Hants, two sides of the box have a quaintly carved human face with open lips, which serve as the money slots, one figure perhaps appropriately putting his tongue out.

There are two examples of a medieval stone receptacle for the offerings of the faithful adjoining a bracket for a figure. They are in the neighbouring churches (of rather different size) of Bridlington Priory and Speeton, East Riding. Seventeenth-century collecting boxes or shovels still exist at Blickling, Norfolk, Nutfield, Surrey, and Whaddon, Bucks.

CHURCH REGISTERS

Medieval churchwardens' accounts are of the greatest possible human interest and value in providing information on church life of the period (St Mary-at-Hill, Eastcheap, City of London). Parish registers for entries of Baptisms, Marriages and Burials were first ordered in 1538, but entry in a book for the purpose was not enjoined until 1598. Wing, Bucks, has perfect and complete registers from 1546.

Just think of all the history and the joy and sorrow that is hidden away in these humble records of life connected with our old churches.

ORIENTATION

Old churches invariably follow approximately a

west to east axis with the altar at the east end. There is, however, often a slight deviation to the north, and much more rarely to the south. The reason for this eastward position is not definitely known. Light comes from the east with the rising sun (sun-worship, possibly), and the Holy Land is in that direction. It was also thought that Our Lord's second coming would be from that quarter.

Occasionally the chancel is not on the same axis as the nave. This is purely accidental and is due to building different parts at different times. This never worried the medieval builder and indeed the result can be pleasing; this in fact is another example of the subtle difference between an old church and a "correct" modern one.

Guide books like to state that such inclined or weeping chancels represent Our Lord's head on the Cross. It is quite incorrect, and in any case chancels weep to the south as well as to the north!

LITURGICAL COLOURS OF THE SEASONS OF THE CHURCH'S YEAR

These apply to the vestments, the chalice veil, the burse (containing the corporal or body cloth, which is spread under the sacred vessels, and there is also a pall, which covers the top of the chalice, and a purificator for cleansing), the altar frontal, and sometimes there is a pulpit cloth or fall.

White Signifies joy, purity and triumph, and is used on feasts of Our Lord, the Blessed Virgin Mary, angels, and saints who were not martyrs (and also during Eastertide and on Trinity Sunday and All Saints' day, 1st November).

Red, being associated with fire, is used at Whitsun, and, being the colour of blood, is used on feasts of martyrs.

Violet is the penitential colour and is used in Advent and Lent (and on the three preceding Sundays), and on Rogation and Ember days. (Rose pink can, however, be used on the third Sunday in Advent and on the fourth Sunday in Lent.)

Green, the colour of nature, is used on Sundays throughout the seasons of Epiphany and Trinity, and on weekdays on which no special feast or fast is being kept. It signifies life and hope.

Black is worn on Good Friday and All Souls' day (2nd November) and for funerals and requiems.

INSTRUMENTS OF THE PASSION

They comprise the crown of thorns, ladder, three nails, hammer, pincers, scourges, whipping pillar, cords, lantern, three dice, seamless robe, spear, basin, sponge on a reed (which was held up to Our Lord), thirty pieces of silver or a bag of silver, cock, jug of vinegar, and the fist that buffeted Him. (The Five Wounds are often shown in this connection.)

EMBLEMS OF THE TWELVE APOSTLES

St Peter	keys
St Andrew	cross saltire (X shaped)
St John the Evangelist	chalice with dragon emerging
St James Major	scallop shell and pilgrim's staff
St Thomas	spear
St James Minor	fuller's club (a long club with a bend at one end)
St Philip	loaves or basket of loaves
St Bartholomew	flaying knife
St Matthias	axe (or sword or scimitar)
St Simon	fish (or saw or oar)
St Jude	boat
St Matthew	sword or scimitar (or axe)
St Paul	sword

SYMBOLS OF THE FOUR EVANGELISTS

St Matthew	angel
St Mark	lion
St Luke	ox
St John	eagle

THE FOUR LATIN DOCTORS

St Gregory	pope in tiara
St Jerome	cardinal
St Augustine	bishop or doctor
St Ambrose	bishop

EMBLEMS OF SOME OTHER
"POPULAR" SAINTS

St John the Baptist	Lamb of God on a book
St Michael, St George and St Margaret	dragon
St Lawrence	gridiron
St Stephen	stones
St Anthony	pig
St Edmund	arrow
St Catherine of Alexandria	wheel
St Mary Magdalene	vase of ointment
St Apollonia	tooth in pincers
St Dorothy	basket of flowers
St Barbara	tower
St Edward the Confessor	holds a ring
St Clement	anchor
St Leonard	chains

SACRED MONOGRAMS

IHC or IHS   abbreviated Greek for Jesus

XP or XPC   abbreviated Greek for Christ

INRI   Latin initials for Jesus of Nazareth, King of the Jews

A fish was an early Christian symbol because the initial letters of the Greek words for Jesus Christ Son of God Saviour form the Greek word for fish.

A lamb with a halo and a banner represents the Lamb of God (Christ) (Agnus Dei)

CONCLUSION

It is hoped that the reader will now have some idea not only of the beauty of our old churches but also of their great number and the immense amount to be seen in each. No other country can compare with England in this respect, and no other country has such a display of church towers. We were always striving after a style of our own and we succeeded in our Perpendicular towers and fan vaults which are unknown anywhere else. In England dignity, reverence and simplicity are usually the key-notes.

We have tried to give a comprehensive account of this great heritage, and anyone able to visit all the examples mentioned, or even a majority of them, should acquire not only useful knowledge but also many happy memories.

No two churches are exactly alike, and it is this fact that makes visiting them such a joy—to discover the one or perhaps two features not found anywhere else.

Entering an old church is always exciting; we give three examples: Great Paxton, Hunts, is an ordinary medieval church outside, but inside one discovers that it is one of our finest Saxon churches; Ickleton, Cambs, has amazing Roman monolith piers; and Hannington, Northants, looks very ordinary outside, but its interior is exceptional in having a double nave.

Quite apart from each church having something different from any other, there will often be oddities. For example, at Kislingbury, Northants, there are eight fire buckets dated 1743, and at Worlingworth,

Suffolk, even the old manual fire engine of 1760 is in the church. Long fire-hooks for pulling down burning thatch will also occasionally be found. At Fenny Stratford, Bucks, can be seen the Fenny poppers—six popgun cannons for explosives still used on St Martin's Day.

Leominster Priory, Herefords, has a ducking-stool, and Alwington, Devon, its stocks.

We have seen that heraldry is extensively used at all times. On capitals at Cogenhoe, Northants, are shields of the thirteenth century which are narrow, as quartering had not then been introduced. In almost the next parish, Easton Maudit, is a coat of Arms on a monument which has over one hundred quarterings.

We have attempted to include everything connected with an old church. No mention has yet been made, however, of anchorite cells. These were very small apartments which were in effect the walling-up for life of the anchorite. These cells were situated on the cold north side of the chancel with one aperture to the High Altar and another aperture to the grave prepared in readiness outside. The form of service of such walling-up is known and there is definite evidence of such structures, more particularly in the south of England: Compton and Shere in Surrey are examples. At Compton there is also a unique Norman upper chancel used probably by pilgrims on the Pilgrims' Way. It has a Norman wooden screen which is the oldest in England.

Large Perpendicular clerestory windows make a splendid exterior, as at Bath Abbey, Somerset, Sherborne Abbey, Dorset, Melton Mowbray,

Leics (Pl. 10), Stonham Aspall, Suffolk and Quadring, Lincs (see p. 15).

Two churches together in the same churchyard can sometimes be found, particularly in the east of England. At Reepham, Norfolk, three churches shared the same churchyard. Soil may be a reason. Often one of the churches is now in ruins, as at South Walsham, Norfolk, but at Willingale Doe and Willingale Spain, Essex, and Trimley, Suffolk, both churches are in use. Each was probably in a separate parish, merely sharing the churchyard. The parochial system is still as strong as ever today. Every little community loves its old church and will not usually travel to the next village to worship; this is a fortunate factor as it does help to keep our heritage intact.

The secret of this heritage is not really in the great and magnificent churches and fittings, but in the innumerable simple and unknown structures with quaint and odd fittings. The illustration of the interior of Puxton, Somerset (Pl. 44), noted for its leaning tower, will help to give the reader some idea of such a church. See p. 122.

We conclude by mentioning some special glories of East Anglia: Sall, Walpole St Peter (Pl. 42), Terrington St Clement, Cawston, Blakeney and Cley, Norfolk, and Lavenham, Long Melford, Blythburgh (Pl. 7) and Southwold (Pl. 7), Suffolk, and on a smaller scale, we must mention Shelton, Wighton, Upton and Swanton Morley, Norfolk, and Denston (Pl. 44) and Little Waldingfield, Suffolk. The mere size alone lifts one out of oneself. The primary object of the medieval builder was to erect a building to the glory of God and His worship, and to express worthily man's belief in the majesty and greatness of God. The screen was not a barrier, but a guide and formed one composition with loft, rood and Doom, the saints painted in the panels below leading to Christ Triumphant above.

Churches which contain nearly all their original features and fittings are always a joy to visit, and in this category we place Woolpit, Ufford, Barking, Kedington, Dennington and Westhall, Suffolk, Edlesborough, Bucks, Houghton Conquest, Beds, Swimbridge, Devon, Banwell, Trull and Monk-silver, Somerset, Lanreath and Altarnun (Pl. 44), Cornwall, and East Markham, Notts. There is even more joy when such a church has all such possessions and is itself quite unrestored. We call to mind South Burlingham, and South Acre, Norfolk, Stoke Dry, Rutland, Stanford, Northants, Graveney, Kent, and Launcells, Cornwall.

Nature provides its own colours outside; no scene can be more beautiful than an English village in springtime. It is hoped that there will be appropriate colour inside the church, such as can be seen at Blisland, Cornwall, and Harberton, Devon. Thaxted, Essex, is also well known in this respect.

An interior that has now been beautifully restored and is an example of what can be done is at Hasel-bury Bryan, Dorset. The interiors of Horley, Oxon, North Cerney, Glos, Torbryan, Devon, Mullion, Cornwall, South Creake, Norfolk, and Egmanton and Holme, Notts, are also very lovely with an atmosphere of devotion. Lound, Suffolk, is full of beauty.

Finally we mention fifteen of England's prettiest villages. It so happens that in each the old church is the making of the picture: Godshill, Isle of Wight, Kersey and Cavendish, Suffolk, Finchingfield and Thaxted, Essex, Chilham, Kent, Castle Combe, Aldbourne and Steeple Ashton, Wilts, Kimbolton, Hunts, Shere, Surrey, South Harting, Sussex, Westmill and Braughing, Herts, and Bishop Burton, East Riding. At Geddington, Northants, the tower and stone spire of the church group splendidly with the Eleanor Cross of 1294 and the old bridge of about the same date.

We have seen that the piety and love for God of past generations have given each village and old town its crowning glory—its old church. We have the privilege of being trustees of this priceless heritage for future generations, who will probably use these churches and appreciate them more than we are doing. Surely we can fulfil that trust and hand them on rather than pull them down. However remote a church may be today, tomorrow it may be in the middle of a New Town or a housing estate. The problem is, of course, a big one, particularly in East Anglia with so many large churches close together and small (but usually very keen) communities.

The Historic Churches Preservation Trust, whose office is at Fulham Palace, London, S.W.6, has the urgent and important task of raising money for the preservation of old churches. The writer stresses the title at his lectures because at one meeting he was introduced as representing the Society for the Prevention of Churches. On another occasion he was referred to as the prehistoric churchman.

Many old churches require thousands of pounds for restoration. Parishes are making heroic efforts and will continue to do so, but sums of this magnitude are quite beyond the resources of small communities. It is the disappearance of wealthy lords of the manor that has caused such a grave crisis in the maintenance of so many country churches. The Trust has therefore had to be established to augment local effort, and this is as it should be, for this heritage belongs to all. The death-watch beetle is the great enemy. He, like the congregation, seems to be encouraged by more warmth today in old churches.

There is also a society called the Friends of Friendless Churches which exists to help save and preserve churches of architectural interest threatened with collapse or demolition and outside the scope or policy of other organizations, the society often bringing back such churches into use.

We must keep the flag flying. It will be seen high above many churches on the great festivals and on the patronal festival. It is the red cross of St George on a white background and it should have the Arms of its diocese in the first quarter.

There is no such thing as an "ordinary" church, for every old church is unique, though all have something in common—the need of man to look beyond himself to something greater, the God of Love and Beauty as revealed by Our Blessed Lord. In each there is worship, the administration of the Sacraments, and the atmosphere of devotion of hundreds of years.

Our glorious churches are of the greatest historic

interest and beauty, but they are not just showpieces. Each is the House of God and the Gate of Heaven in our villages and old towns. The village church with its tower or spire dominates the English scene; pointing upwards to Heaven, it advertises both the fact and the purpose of its existence.

These old churches are today still sermons in stone and living witnesses of the Faith for which they were built, and it is our privilege to use them and preserve them for posterity. Let us do so to the greater glory of God, and thereby also fulfil the true purpose of human life—to love, serve and praise God.

To visit all of them, one must begin in the year one is born, live to a hundred, and visit a hundred a year!

HOW TO DATE A BRASS

The illustrations on the following pages are a complete record from the thirteenth century to the seventeenth century of every type of armour, civil costume and ladies' dresses and head-dresses, together with the different types of ecclesiastical vestments, monks' and nuns' habits and academical and judicial costume. (For text references see pages 144 to 150.)

Acton, Suffolk, 1302: armour to 1305.

Westley Waterless, Cambs, 1325: 1305 to 1350.

Sawtry, Hunts, 1404: armour 1350 to 1410, dress 1390 to 1430.

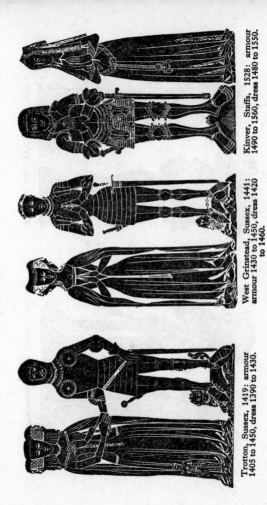

Kinver, Staffs, 1528; armour
1490 to 1560, dress 1480 to 1550.

West Grinstead, Sussex, 1441:
armour 1430 to 1450, dress 1420
to 1460.

Trotton, Sussex, 1419: armour
1405 to 1450, dress 1390 to 1430.

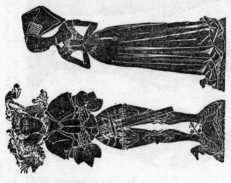

Swinbrook, Oxon, 1470: 1450 to 1480.

Ulcombe, Kent, 1470: 1460 to 1500.

East Sutton, Kent, 1629: armour 1625 to 1660, dress 1600 to 1660, civilians (sons) 1600 to 1660.

Upton, Bucks, 1599: 1570 to 1625.

Morley, Derbyshire, 1558: armour 1540 to 1570, dress 1540 to 1580.

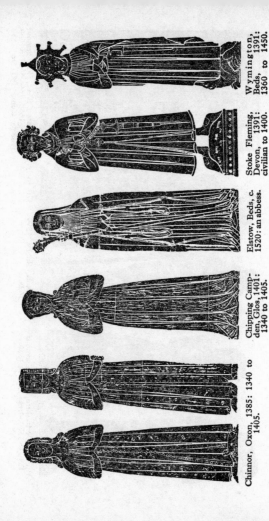

Wymington, Beds, 1391: 1360 to 1450.

Stoke Fleming, Devon, 1391: civilian to 1400.

Elstow, Beds, c. 1520: an abbess.

Chipping Campden, Glos, 1401: 1340 to 1405.

Chinnor, Oxon, 1385: 1340 to 1405.

Brightwell Baldwin, Oxon, 1439: a judge, ladies' dress 1420 to 1450.

Whitchurch, Hants, 1603: civilian 1550 to 1625, ladies' dress 1570 to 1625.

Witney, Oxon, 1501:
1475 to 1560.

Great Linford, Bucks,
1473: 1440 to 1485.

Thorncombe, Dorset, 1437: 1420 to
1460.

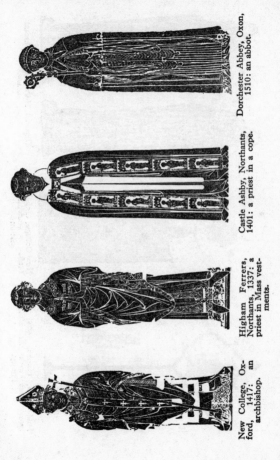

New College, Oxford, 1417: an archbishop.

Higham Ferrers, Northants, 1337: a priest in Mass vestments.

Castle Ashby, Northants, 1401: a priest in a cope.

Dorchester Abbey, Oxon, 1510: an abbot.

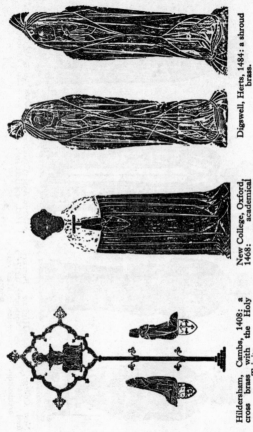

Digswell, Herts, 1484: a shroud brass.

New College, Oxford, 1468: academical costume.

Hildersham, Cambs, 1408: a cross brass with the Holy Trinity.

CANTERBURY.   YORK.

Coats of Arms of the two provinces of the Church of England.

APPENDIX OF ADDITIONAL
EXAMPLES

West Country Rood-screens Dunchideock, Harberton, Swimbridge, Chawleigh and King's Nympton, Devon, and High Ham and Halse, Somerset.

Figure Paintings on South Devon Screens Torbryan, Plymtree, Wolborough, Kenn, Bradninch, Holne, Buckland-in-the-Moor, Ugborough, East Portlemouth, Chudleigh, Ipplepen, Bovey Tracey and Hennock, Bridford has small carved figures.

Rood-Lofts Atherington, Devon, Avebury, Wilts, St Margaret's, Herefords, Cotes-by-Stow, Lincs, Hubberholme, West Riding and Dennington, Suffolk (parcloses).

Stalls Tabernacled canopies, in order of date: Lancaster, Lincoln, Chester, Nantwich, Carlisle, Ripon, Manchester and Beverley Minster. Parish church stalls: Higham Ferrers, Northants, Stowlangtoft, Southwold and Wingfield, Suffolk, Balsham, Cambs, and Minster-in-Thanet, Kent.

Misericords Nantwich, Cheshire, Great Malvern Priory, Worcs, Higham Ferrers, Northants, Sherborne Abbey, Dorset, Cartmel Priory and Whalley, Lancs, and Minster-in-Thanet, Kent.

Wall-paintings Black Bourton and South Newington, Oxon, Easby, North Riding, Claverley, Salop, West Chiltington, Sussex, Idsworth,

Hants, Peakirk and Slapton, Northants, Bartlow, Cambs, and Haddon Hall Chapel, Derbyshire.

Stained glass 13th century: Madley, Herefords; 14th century: Wells Cathedral, Kempsey, Worcs; 15th century: Ludlow, Salop, and in the Chapels of New College and All Souls' College, Oxford. Passion scenes: East Brent, Somerset, and St Kew, Cornwall.

Note: coloured glass was produced as pot-metal from the melting pot and was coloured throughout, but ruby was usually coated on to white glass for lightness.

Emblem of the Holy Trinity (The Holy Trinity is also shown by the seated Father holding the crucified Son, a dove being above the cross.)

FURTHER BOOKS TO READ

by the author

Enjoying Historic Churches, published by S.P.C.K. It has 14 colour plates and 12 monochrome plates, and text which forms a general introduction to the subject. The Foreword is by the Archbishop of Canterbury.

A Guide to Some Interesting Old English Churches, published by S.P.C.K. This is a list with full details of all the most noteworthy churches arranged under counties. 2 colour plates and 4 monochrome plates.

For detailed references to points of interest in each church in a particular county, we can thoroughly recommend the Penguin Books *Buildings of England* Series by Nikolaus Pevsner, Methuen's *Little Guides*, and Hodder and Stoughton's *King's England* Series by Arthur Mee.

Collins's *Guide to English Parish Churches* (2 vols.) edited by Sir John Betjeman, lists churches of note of all dates under counties.

INDEX OF ILLUSTRATIONS

MAP SHOWING
LOCAL BUILDING
MATERIALS

· SOMERSET

North Petherton

Mells

Bishop's Lydeard

St. Mary Magdalene Taunton

Dundry

Bleadon

Chew Magna